'As I see it, it was the beautiful, wild, to-hell-with-you 16th that did it at Omaha. Its soldiers walked through the minefields, took out German fortifications and seized the bluffs...'

Bill Friedman in the Foreword to
Omaha Beach: V Corps Battle for the Beachhead

This present book is about some of those men.
I am interested in them particularly for a number of reasons, the most obvious being that for seven months in 1943-44 they lived in West Dorset where I now live. During the war I was only a schoolboy in the north of England, excited by what was going on, but mainly interested in collecting shrapnel. Now, in retirement, I am able to think about those days more deeply and the more I do, I am made aware of how very close this country was to disaster. It is certain that without the help of men like those of the 16th Infantry, we would have lost the war. This fact has made a deep impression on me and my feelings concerning our debt to the young Americans who trained here in Britain at that time.

ROBIN PEARCE was born near Barnsley in Yorkshire in 1934. After leaving school he worked at the Atomic Energy Research Establishment at Harwell. In 1953 he was called up for National Service, where he studied Russian and served as a Leading Coder (Special) in the Royal Navy. In 1955 he decided to become a teacher and for thirty-six years taught Religious Studies, History and Archaeology in secondary schools. Five years ago he began research into the crash in 1943 of a German bomber in Beaminster, research which resulted in his highly successful book about the incident, *Operation Wasservogel*, and which led him to a wider study of military history.

16TH INFANTRY REGIMENT

Seven Months to D-Day

An American Regiment in Dorset

ROBIN PEARCE

THE DOVECOTE PRESS

To my wife Sheila.
For her constant encouragement in the research,
her companionship in the fieldwork,
and for helping with the book.

Postcard showing Beaminster at the time the Americans were here. Into a community
with a population of about 1600 there suddenly arrived about 600 soldiers with all
their vehicles and equipment. They were momentous days! The postcard was sent to
his home in the States by Roger Julson, a member of the Anti-Tank Company. The
town's name has been scratched out by the army censor.

First published in 2000 by The Dovecote Press Ltd
Stanbridge, Wimborne, Dorset BH21 4JD

ISBN 1 874336 84 9

Text © Robin T. Pearce 2000

Designed and produced by The Dovecote Press Ltd
Printed and bound by the Baskerville Press, Salisbury

A CIP catalogue record of this book is
available from the British Library

1 3 5 7 9 8 6 4 2

Contents

Introduction 6

Governors Island 8

The Regiment 11

Headquarters 15

1st Battalion 25

2nd Battalion 35

3rd Battalion 43

Anti-Tank Company 50

Cannon Company 57

Marshalling Areas 65

Embarkation 71

Omaha Beach 75

Appendices 79

Glossary 82

Further Reading 83

Acknowledgements 84

Index 85

Introduction

Apart from the small number of people who were alive when the United States Army came to Dorset, there are few who realize the extent of the 'invasion'. Several books have been published which tell the story of the seven or so months before D-Day, but most of them do not go into specific detail about where the Americans were and how they spent their time. In this present book I have put together some of the information I have been given by GI veterans and a number of local residents. Over a span of 55 years memories fade and some of my contacts cannot agree on some locations and dates. For this reason, confirmation has been sought in official documents and primary sources.

The study is confined to West Dorset because that is where the 16th Infantry Regiment was based. A study of this kind devoted to a wider area would be difficult to handle. Also, it is felt that a good picture of the war situation can be given using only a limited number of witnesses over a limited area. In other words, this book is an attempt to show what it was like in Beaminster or Lyme Regis or any of the other small villages where the regiment was to be found.

Photographs have been included, but they tend to be of a poor quality. The Americans were told not to take photographs, though many did, but the size of the film used and the type of cameras available meant that many of the pictures were too small and not properly focused and the civilian population found it difficult to obtain film. The best photographs of that period were taken either by civilian professionals or the Army itself.

Official photographs were taken in the Weymouth area and around Burton Bradstock where members of the 3113 Signals Service Battalion and the 3252 Signals Service Company were based.

Contact was made with members of the 16th Infantry largely through the Internet. In fact, without this speedy means of communication progress would have been very slow. Using e-mail, brief questions could be sent quickly and cheaply and replies received almost straight away. The veterans all volunteered to write to me in response to a notice in the Regiment's magazine *Dagwood Dispatches*. It might be argued, therefore, that the results of the research are likely to be unbalanced since the veterans who co-operated in the venture would have been nice, friendly people. The unpleasant types and trouble-makers would not have replied to the invitation. All I can say in reply is that the local residents

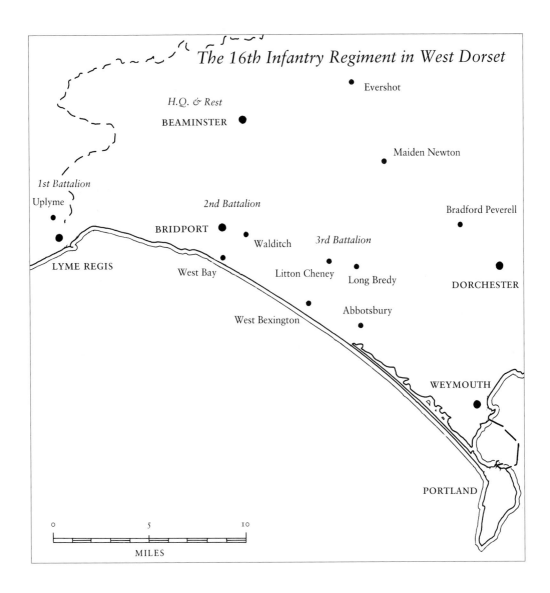

The 16th Infantry Regiment in West Dorset

Evershot

H.Q. & Rest
BEAMINSTER

Maiden Newton

1st Battalion
Uplyme

2nd Battalion

Bradford Peverell

BRIDPORT

Walditch   *3rd Battalion*

LYME REGIS

West Bay   Litton Cheney
Long Bredy   DORCHESTER

West Bexington   Abbotsbury

WEYMOUTH

PORTLAND

0   5   10
MILES

who had daily contact with the Americans described them as well-behaved, friendly and generous. They were not all perfect, but the community into which they came to live was not perfect either.

ROBIN PEARCE
Mosterton, October 2000

ONE

Governors Island

For most of the time between the two World Wars, the 16th Infantry Regiment was based at Fort Jay on Governors Island, which lies at the entrance to New York harbour. From 1698, the English governor of New York used the island for his residence until it was captured by the American forces in 1783. The Americans built Fort Jay on the island in 1798 for the protection of New York.

During the First World War, the regiment fought in France and German. The recognition of their effectiveness in battle by the French is shown by the right they gave to the 16th Infantry to wear the *fourragère*. This was a representation of the *Croix de Guerre*. People in Dorset commented on this ornamental cord with its brass pendant worn by soldiers with their best Class 'A' uniforms. The Americans also liberated the town of Fléville in the wooded Argonne region of France in October 1918. For this they were given the right to wear the *vair*, the alternate lines of blue and white on the heraldic arms of the town. It now forms the background of the regiment's badge which can be seen at the front of this book.

In December 1940, the 3rd Battalion left Fort Jay for Edgewood Arsenal to practice amphibious landings. Later they went to Culebra, an island off Puerto Rico for further landings with the 3rd Battalion of the 18th Infantry. On completion of the training the two Infantry Battalions sailed to Boston and Fort Devens, Massachusetts, where new cantonment barracks had been built. The whole 1st Division was able to assemble there. By then many of those who were to serve in West Dorset had joined the regiment. More practice landings were made at Buzzards Bay off Cape Cod and New Berne in North Carolina. The 1st Division then moved to Camp Blanding in Florida. Private Bruce LaRose from Bethlehem, Pennsylvania, was one of them.

Bruce LaRose had signed up at Fort Jay in December 1940 at the age of eighteeen. Three years later he came to Beaminster with Cannon Company. One assignment Bruce was given involved the testing of a new battle uniform for the army. He and two other soldiers were sent to Harvard University, near Boston in Massachusetts, to take part in tests. They had blood pressure, body temperature and pulse rate monitored as they were put through stress tests in the laboratory. Presumably some of the information gained was put to use in the design of later uniforms.

The final move before embarkation was to the 17,000 acres of training

Private Bruce A. LaRose with a machine-gun at Camp Blanding in Florida
on the 1000 inch range.

facilities at Fort Indiantown Gap in Pennsylvania. From there the 1st Division
was taken to New York where they boarded the *Queen Mary* for the hazardous
crossing to Glasgow. This was no luxury cruise. The liner was serving as a troop-
ship and sleeping accommodation was cramped. On August 7, 1942 they
disembarked at Gourock in the Firth of Clyde, about 20 miles west of Glasgow.
They were then taken down to Tidworth Camp in Wiltshire where they prepared
for the invasion of North Africa.

For about two months they trained for amphibious landings with British
commandos and US Rangers. Then, in October 1942, they embarked on HMS
Warwick Castle and HMS *Duchess of Bedford* for the voyage to the Gulf of
Arzew in Algeria. The landing took place on November 8. Mistakes were made
and lessons were learnt. The African campaign lasted about six months until
May 1943.

After that, preparations were made for the invasion of Sicily which took place
in July, and where the regiment experienced powerful resistance from the
Germans. In particular they had to face the elite *Hermann Göring Panzer
Division*. It was there that the regiment's Cannon Company fought very
effectively. With accurate firing from the 105 mm howitzers, the German
onslaught was stopped. It was one of the decisive battles of the Sicilian
campaign. A few months later some of these howitzers would be parked in

Private Joe Morrisey of the 16th Infantry outside the Red Lion Hotel in Beaminster. The seven month period in Dorset was for many the happiest part of the war.

Beaminster at the top of Fleet Street with the trucks that towed them. There is still an open space at Newtown where the motor pool used to be.

The regiment advanced northwards across Sicily from Niscemi to Troina. During this period a new Commanding Officer was appointed to the 1st Division. He was Major General Clarence Huebner, a strict disciplinarian. His leadership brought a level of discipline to the regiment which was noticed by the people they met in West Dorset.

When they were given a period of rest, the battle-hardened troops enjoyed the Sicilian autumn sunshine. Across the Straits of Messina, Italy was still held by a powerful German army. Many expected that they would be involved in the invasion of Italy, but when the order was given to pack up the equipment in crates, they knew they would be going elsewhere. They hoped that it would be home to the United States, but they were soon disillusioned and found themselves heading for Dorset. Late in October they embarked for the long voyage to Liverpool. They arrived there late on November 5 and were marched to the railway station. Quite a lot of civilians had turned out to watch them go past, but the Americans were prevented from saying anything to them by the lines of Military Police on either side. In carriages with covered windows they travelled to Dorchester in Dorset. On the ship they had been told to remove the divisional insignia from their uniforms – the 'Big Red One'. The authorities did not want German spies to find out about this elite regiment's presence in Dorset.

TWO

The Regiment

The 16th Infantry Regiment was part of the 1st Infantry Division. This Division of about 14000 men was based in Dorset. The Divisional headquarters were at Langton House in the village of Langton Long Blandford, about a mile south-east of Blandford Forum. There were two other Infantry Regiments within the Division: the 18th Infantry Regiment based in central Dorset and the 26th Infantry Regiment based in east Dorset. The 16th Infantry was in the west and had its headquarters at Parnham House, Beaminster. The 18th had its headquarters at Ilsington House, Puddletown, and the 26th at Binnegar Hall, East Stoke, near Wareham.

The structure of each of these regiments was the same. First, about a hundred men formed the Headquarters and Headquarters Company. In the case of the 16th Infantry, the Headquarters Staff lived in Parnham House and other billets nearby. The Headquarters Company, which included a wide range of specialists, from cooks to 'Intelligence and Reconnaissance' platoons, were in Quonset huts in the grounds of Parnham House and in fields across the Bridport road.

There were also three Infantry Battalions, each of which consisted of four Companies as well as its own Headquarters Company. The 1st Battalion was based in the Lyme Regis area. The 2nd Battalion was based in the Bridport area and the 3rd Battalion was based in a number of small villages between Abbotsbury and Litton Cheney.

1st Battalion: Companies A, B, C, D + Headquarters
2nd Battalion: Companies E, F, G, H + Headquarters
3rd Battalion: Companies I, K, L, M + Headquarters

These Companies each had three platoons of riflemen and one further platoon which dealt with heavy weapons. A captain and four junior officers led the Company. The Battalion's Headquarters Company also had a Headquarters Section, an Ammunition and Pioneer platoon, a Communications platoon and an Anti-Tank platoon. In addition the regiment had a Medical Section and Communications Platoon (Radio Section, Wire Section and Message Centre). The Service Company had a Personnel Section. A total of over 3000 men of the 16th Infantry were based in West Dorset.

Parnham House, Beaminster, the Headquarters of the 16th Infantry Regiment.

They trained in the fields and woods of the county and would also go to amphibious training areas in Devon at Woolacombe, Braunton and also Slapton Sands, near Tor Cross. Live ammunition was used and soldiers were sometimes killed accidentally.

The troops returned to England from Sicily dressed in olive-drab field jackets and trousers (known as 'ODs') with open-necked shirts. The uniforms were made of wool. They also had knitted caps, jumpers and scarves On their feet they had leather boots and long gaiters (also known as 'leggings'). As all items of equipment were stamped 'Government Issue', the soldiers were known as GIs. Infantrymen were also known as 'Doughboys'.

Few had the 1st Division badge on their left shoulders. These were put on for the invasion, but for much of the time the authorities wanted the units to be anonymous. The Germans would become suspicious if an elite unit like the 1st Division was in Dorset. British intelligence had used several ways to persuade the enemy that the main thrust would come from the south-east where the fictitious First US Army Group (FUSAG) was supposed to be based (see chapter 10).

As the Companies were scattered and in some cases the men were in billets spread over a wide area, the usual parades in the morning at Reveille and in the

Ilsington House, Puddletown, was the Headquarters of the 18th Infantry Regiment.

evenings at Retreat were not always organized. On the other hand, where men could be assembled easily, these formations were held. In Lyme Regis, for example, the local population would turn out to see the soldiers fall in for Retreat formations in Woodmead Road and at the bottom of Broad Street. In Beaminster also, people would watch them in the Square and in East Street. Rachel Bowditch recalls seeing them lined up in East Street as she walked to school and seeing them still there in the afternoon.

Large formal parades with flags and pennants (see illustration on page 56) were seldom held. Two exceptions were when Montgomery and Eisenhower came to address the regiment.

The US Army was segregated. Few black soldiers were seen in Beaminster, Bridport or Lyme Regis. Similarly, where there were black units it was unusual to see white troops. Conflict sometimes arose when these boundaries were crossed in off-duty time. Two sergeants from the 1st Battalion, for instance, got into a fight when they went into a 'black' pub for a drink. They were arrested by MPs and subsequently 'busted' for the action. This incident probably took place in Maiden Newton where there was a black Quartermaster Troop. It was from there that bread and refrigerated food was delivered to the regiment. Cecil Poole, a Special Constable at Beaminster Police Station, was left in charge one night when the Military Police and Sergeant Neal were called out to Evershot. There was a fight involving black troops.

The 16th Infantry soon settled down to life in this quiet part of Dorset. Many friendships were formed with civilians, and young Americans far away from home found new homes from home here. As Perry Bonner of Cannon Company put it, 'The people in Beaminster were the best people in the world.' Doris Britton, a young Land Army Girl in Beaminster said, 'Those GIs were such a part of everyone's life for the seven months.' She got to know many at the Congregational Church in Whitcombe Road.

THREE

Headquarters

Parnham House in Beaminster was owned by Eric Bullivant when the Americans went there. He and his wife lived in part of the house and his daughter lived in a house in the grounds. The senior officers slept upstairs in the house and junior staff lived nearby in Quonsets (see *Glossary*). Rooms downstairs were used for administration and dining. A large attic bedroom was used for the detailed planning of the Omaha Beach landings. The staircase leading to this room was always guarded.

After many months of fighting in Africa and Sicily they found Parnham 'a heaven, a bucolic delight of a place we had seen in pictures, but never imagined in reality' (Captain Bill Friedman, Adjutant). The picturesque setting in the valley of the Brit and the panoramic view of beautiful green wooded hills impressed the Americans very much. So too did the old house. 'To have slept in that wonderful Parnham House after the discomforts of the field, to participate in history just by being there was an unforgettable experience for all of us.'

The hilly fields and the hedgerows, the small copses and the more extensive

Colonel Bill Friedman, US Army (retired) on a visit to Beaminster in January, 2000. In 1943 he was Captain Friedman, Adjutant at the regiment's HQ at Parnham House.

Outside Parnham House. Left to right: Colonel Taylor, Lt. Colonel Matthews,
Major Carl Plitt, Major Charles Tegtmyer, Major Lauten.

woodland were appreciated by many of these young men. They were also to be
the scene of intensive training for the bloody conflict only a few months ahead.
The incongruity of the situation was seen clearly one night when General Omar
Bradley was staying at Parnham. Sitting with Bill Friedman in one of the panelled
rooms in the quietness of evening, the General 'told me about the feelings and
fears that he had sending his troops on what he believed would be a terrible and
costly mission.'

The senior staff at the headquarters were:

Colonel George A. Taylor, Commanding Officer
Lt. Colonel John Matthews, Executive Officer
Captain Bill Friedman, S-1 (Adjutant)
Major John Lauten, S-2 (Intelligence, Training)
Captain Carl Plitt, S-3 (Plans and Training)
Major Leonard Godfrey, S-4 (Supply)
Major Charles Tegtmyer, Regimental Surgeon
Father Lawrence Deery, Regimental Chaplain

John Lauten said, 'A major activity in the planning room was assigning

Colonel George A. Taylor, CO of the 16th Infantry in 1944.

'bottoms' (landing craft) for the loading of troops and equipment.' The Division had requisitioned the number needed and the staff at Parnham had to locate them and decide in which order the regiment's troops and equipment would be loaded. Careful plans were drawn up for the moving of vehicles from the marshalling areas to Weymouth. 'They also had to make provision for reporters, cameramen and special liaison personnel.'

One of the staff at Parnham was a talented artist who had worked for Walt Disney Studios before the war. Inspired by the old paintings on the wall of the main hall, he did caricatures of four of the staff dressed in period costume to match the other paintings. Colonel Taylor was portrayed as King Arthur with a baseball bat as a sceptre. Major Lauten was Merlin holding a crystal ball. The other two officers were also members of the Court of King Arthur. The pictures were about a metre high and were suitably framed and hung on the hall wall. They disappeared after the regiment left for Normandy. Colonel Taylor's helmet bears the eagle badge of a full colonel (sometimes known as a 'bird' colonel).

Corporal Samuel Fuller was also in Headquarters Company. He went on to become a film director after the war and in 1980 produced the film *The Big Red One* starring Lee Marvin. Fuller also contributed to Lieutenant John Baumgartner's *History of the 16th Infantry Regiment*.

The Headquarters Staff came from a wide variety of backgrounds. John Lauten, for instance, was a lawyer and had been Deputy City Attorney for Glendale when, as a member of the Reserve Officers Training Corps (ROTC), he was called up for service at Fort Benning. After the war he became City Attorney for Fresno and then the General Manager of the State Water Authority in California.

The Jeep was probably the most commonly seen army vehicle in Beaminster. They were frequently parked in and around the Square. Rachel Bowditch, on her way to school, remembers seeing one Jeep in particular which was parked under the arch near the entrance to Fleet Street. On the back it had the word 'Lee'. The name stuck in her imagination and she decided that when she was married, if she had a son, she would call him Lee. Some years later she named her son Lee.

At Parnham House there were the Jeeps of the 'Intelligence and Reconnaissance' Platoon. They had 'IR' painted on the front bumper. As Joe Rowley put it, these platoons were the 'eyes and ears' of Major Lauten. In battle they would go ahead of the main body of troops searching out the enemy. Often they could be miles ahead of the rest. They would radio back information about enemy positions so that they could be attacked by artillery and mortars. These platoons were heavily armed. They had 'four machine guns, plus tommy guns, bazookas, 60 mm mortars, and assorted rifles and pistols.' They were engaged in dangerous operations. Joe was wounded in the Battle of the Bulge and was awarded the Purple Heart.

When Montgomery visited Bridport to speak to the 16th Infantry, Joe was ordered to clean his 'I and R' Jeep so that Monty could use it. The Americans knew that Monty would often speak to the troops from the bonnet of a vehicle. The grass was wet in the large meadow near West Bay and so when Monty climbed on the seat to step out onto the bonnet, he left muddy foot marks. Joe was not very pleased!

The regiment had gone to some trouble in preparing for the visit. There had been much marching and drilling. The orderly parade, however, became chaotic when Monty told the soldiers to gather around the Jeep and take their hats off so that he could see them better. Another break from routine was the announcement from the General that they could have the rest of the day off. When Eisenhower came on another occasion the parade was formal and no time off was given.

John Bistrica of 'C' Company based at Lyme Regis was a Jeep driver who often drove for the heavy weapons platoon. Not being used to the black-out he missed

Sergeant Joseph Rowley at the wheel of one of the 'I and R' (Intelligence and Reconnaissance) Jeeps at Parnham House. Demetrius Lypka is holding the barrel of the heavy machine-gun.

a turning and ran into a hedge. His Commanding Officer said to him, 'That's OK Bistrica, you'll learn.' On another occasion the officer in the Jeep said that he was driving too slowly. Bistrica got out and scraped off some of the paint from the headlight glass which had been put there to reduce the intensity of the light. Soon after that they were stopped by MPs for a violation of the blackout regulations.

Bistrica commented on the blackout on another occasion when he and John Adamcyzk got lost after visiting the canteen early in their time at Lyme. The next day they bought 'flashlights' from the 'hardware store'. He still remembers the English calling them 'torches' and 'ironmongers'.

There was much fun and enjoyment during the seven month period. 'There are

Local children (Reggie Riglar, Jim House, John Page, Peter Page, and Richard Wetherden) sitting on the bonnet of a Jeep in Church Street, Beaminster.

many memories of great parties, wonderful and poignant romances and the kindness of the locals, who bore our antics with a gret deal of patience.' (Bill Friedman) The people of Beaminster also enjoyed the generosity of the soldiers.

The officers ate well, but as John Lauten remembers the furniture they used was basic. 'Our dining table consisted of two six-foot folding tables placed end to end in the centre of the room. It was pretty incongruous.'

Local people were invited to dine with the soldiers in the Public Hall for the celebration of Thanksgiving on November 25, 1943, (the fourth Thursday in November) and at Christmas in 1943. Afterwards the surplus food was given away. Cold roast chicken and ham was eaten for many days afterwards in some homes. Apple pie and cream also found its way to the town from the field kitchens at Parnham.

The Americans also soon enjoyed fish and chips, and the queue in North Street was often mainly of soldiers. When they realized that this was about the only food not rationed and that the people relied on it, they moderated their consumption. The same applied to freshly baked bread and cakes. In fact, after public protest in Lyme Regis, Company 'C' were ordered not to go to the bakery in Broad Street. On the other hand, beer was a different matter! Many pubs ran dry before the end of the week.

Dances were organized in the Public Hall and the regiment had a good band

Private Angelo Macchi outside Parnham House.
He was a cook in Headquarters Company.

Angelo Macchi with an evacuee he sponsored
for the Christmas Party in December 1943.

conducted by Staff Sergeant Kryzanowski. The initials on the musicians' music stands had the initials 'BK'. Americans also went to dances arranged by local organizations such as the Land Army.

The Medical Detachment in Beaminster also helped the civilians when there was a need. Some local people even received dental treatment from the US Army. When the terrible road accident occurred involving Kathleen Stainer Tennant of Ham's Plot, the American doctors were quickly on the scene and with Dr. Lake of Beaminster they gave first aid until an ambulance came to take her to Dorchester. Mrs. Tennant, the daughter of Sir William Alcock, the organist at Salisbury Cathedral was trying a horse for her son and was leaving Furzy Lane to return home along the Bridport road. The horse reared when a large tank

Staff Sergeant Kryzanowski's band playing at a dance in the Public Hall, Beaminster.

Bridge House, Beaminster, where many officers were accommodated.

Parnham House staff during an exercise early in 1944.
Left to right: Colonel George A. Taylor, Major Carl W. Plitt, Major Charles E. Tegtmyer,
Major John Lauten, Captain William Friedman.

transporter went past. Mrs. Tennant was thrown and later died. The transporter was moving slowly up the hill towards Bridport. Several local girls saw the accident. Furzy Lane was popular for walks on a Sunday, especially since it was near the army camp.

Some Americans also went to churches in Beaminster. The Congregational church in Whitcombe Road had lively services with new and tuneful hymns. The minister, Mr. Wheedon, known by some of the Land Girls as 'Woe and Whiskers', chose hymns that the large number of Americans in the congregation liked. This meant that 'The old rugged cross' was often sung along with Moody and Sankey compositions.

The Regimental Chaplain was Father Lawrence 'Larry' Deery, a rough, tough Roman Catholic. He lived in Parnham House and was respected by the other officers. He was courageous in battle and a great help to those who needed him. The night before the landing on Omaha Beach he was on HMS *Empire Anvil* with the first wave troops quietly reading John Addington Symond's *Life of Michelangelo*. Services were held on all the large Landing Ships taking part in the invasion.

The US Military Police worked with the Dorset Police. In the police station

The back of Parnham House, showing the window of the attic bedroom where the plans for the Omaha Beach landing were made.

there were three cells; soldiers getting out of hand were brought there. Those guilty of serious criminal acts were taken to Dorchester. There were some ugly incidents from time to time in various parts of the county and some nasty fights, but generally speaking from what has been reported, the behaviour of the majority of the Americans soldiers was good.

As D-Day approached the training intensified. 'Large unit manoeuvres took place on beaches west of Dorset.' (John Lauten). 'Highly classified officers at each level searched the Dorset area for countryside that was like the that in Normandy and then devised training exercises to utilize the terrain. The hedgerows were a challenge and the movement of small deer demonstrated what could be expected in case of an attack through a wood.' Assault training took place on the north Devon coast in February 1944 and in April what turned into disastrous practice landings took place at Slapton Sands (although the 16th was not involved in the E-boat attack).

Just before the end of May 1944 the order came to leave Beaminster and assemble in the Marshalling Areas nearer to Weymouth. The townspeople knew it would happen, but it still came as a shock. Many romances and many friendships were suddenly interrupted; some never to be resumed.

FOUR

The 1st Battalion

On their return from Sicily the 16th Infantry were pleased to be in a country where English was spoken. They were also delighted by the Dorset countryside and people. It was the 1st Battalion, however, and 'C' Company in particular, who felt themselves lucky to be sent to Lyme Regis. The attractive little town by the 'ocean' with a cinema and variety of pubs seemed idyllic to many of them.

The Commanding Officer of the 1st Battalion was Lieutenant Colonel Bowers. He was older than the other senior staff and Major Driscoll, his Executive Officer, took command of the Battalion just prior to D-Day.

Captain Charles M. Hangsterfer (*see the photograph below*) was the Commanding Officer of the Headquarters Company of the 1st Battalion at Lyme Regis and also the Battalion Adjutant. He was a graduate of the historic Gettysburg College and a member of the Reserve Officers Training Corps. After further military training, including a communications course at Fort Benning in Georgia, he joined the 16th Infantry and specialized in communications. He had a good sense of humour. When General Omar Bradley addressed a meeting of all

Summerhill, Lyme Regis. The house, which has since been demolished, served as HQ for the 1st Battalion. From 1923-27 it had been used by the Scottish educationalist A.S. Neill as a school.

the regimental officers he told them that he would have given anything to go with them. Hank said, 'I was going to offer him a place in the LCVP for twenty bucks, but reconsidered.'

Known as 'lovable Hank', he was respected by his men. He was strong on discipline, but also showed care for those who needed it. Bob Guiser, for instance, had been a radio operator in North Africa and Sicily and had received severe back injuries. It was no longer possible for him to carry a heavy radio and so he was made a 'runner' on Omaha Beach. In Lyme Regis he was also excused much of the training and given the job of washing dishes at the NAAFI canteen not far from the Guildhall and overlooking the sea.

Guiser remembers fetching jam tarts from the bakery each morning for the canteen. Hank also made him Company bugler and Bob would go off to a quiet spot in the remote woodland above Lyme Regis to practise. On an amphibious landing exercise, Guiser's bugle was broken and so his Reveille and Retreat were not heard any more.

Some of the soldiers had suffered 'combat fatigue' after their experiences in Africa and Sicily. As they did not want to leave the battalion, Hank used them as 'road guides and protection for the Battalion Command Post'. He referred to them as his 'MP Platoon'.

As the training intensified and plans were explained at further meetings, Hank pointed out that the proposal for a daylight landing in Normandy came as a great shock. Previous landings had been at night. They were told that their

Looking down Silver Street in Lyme Regis. The white house on the left was 'C' Company HQ. Further down on the right is the Dorset Hotel which was a billet for the Medical Detachment.

superior fire power and the bombing and shelling would give them a great advantage over what was thought to be a second-rate German division.

'C' Company was billeted in houses and hotels in the town. When they first arrived they spent two weeks in tents. The headquarters of 'C' Company were on the corner of Silver Street and Woodmead Road. The house now has a plaque on the wall which was placed there by John Bistrica from Youngstown, Ohio, and Frederick Erben from Lindenhurst, New York. They had both become very

John Bistrica and Frederick Erben with the bronze plaque they placed on the house that had been 'C' Company's HQ. John Bistrica was made a 'Distinguished Member of the Regiment' by the Secretary of the Army in 1997 for his efforts to contact veterans.

AT THIS SITE, NOV. 1943 TO JUNE 1944, WAS LOCATED THE HEADQUARTERS OF "C" CO., 16TH INF. REGT., 1ST U.S. INF. DIV. WHO LEAD THE ASSAULT LANDING AT OMAHA BEACH ON D-DAY (JUNE 6, 1944) IN NORMANDY, FRANCE. CAPT. VICTOR H. BRIGGS, C.O.

Weapons Platoon of 'C' Company in Lyme Regis just before D-Day.
Joseph Dragotto is second from the right on the back row.

attached to the people of the town and still exchange visits. Mrs. Way who lived in Woodmead Road next door to their billet became a mother to these young men. Fred recalls, 'She used to chastise me for my jaunty ways and habits.' Mrs. Way's youngest son became the Company mascot and a special US Army uniform was made for him.

John Bistrica was a Catholic and went to mass at the church of St. Michael and St. George with other soldiers. Before they left for Normandy they presented a monstrance to the church. Another devout Catholic in the Company was Joseph Dragotto from Utica, New York. There was an incident later on in the war which troubled his Christian conscience. He was on the edge of Cologne when he received an order from the Company Command Post to go into the town to get some candles. Knowing that a church would be the most likely place to have candles, he took three men in a Jeep and approached the cathedral. Inside they found several candles, including the large Paschal candle. As he was leaving he knelt to ask forgiveness for the act. In his brief unpublished memoirs he wrote: 'I prayed, dear God, I am sorry, but we need these candles more than you do . . .'.

Joe was also involved in a tragic happening at another Catholic church in Belgium on Christmas Eve in 1944. Several GIs had gone to Midnight Mass at a village church. They had taken presents for the children. As they drove away

The Chalet, Lyme Regis (later demolished after a landslip). This building was the sleeping accommodation of the Battalion CO and his staff.

from the church, they heard the familiar drone of a 'Doodlebug', the pilotless aircraft known as the V-1. Suddenly the engine cut out and it fell to the ground hitting the church. The men rushed back to do what they could. Many had been killed.

The 1st Battalion's other three rifle Companies were billeted to the north of the town either in Quonset huts or private houses. Company 'D' lived in huts in a large field above The Spittles to the east of Lyme. The Company officers were accommodated in the Hotel Alexandra in the town and the Commanding Officer and Battalion staff in The Chalet. The St. Michael's Hotel was used as the Battalion officers' mess. There was also an unwritten agreement that the Three Cups Hotel was to be used by officers only. The enlisted men used other pubs in the town. Joseph Dragotto said, 'The people of the town were wonderful; they treated us like part of the town. They even gave us a pub to use as our own. We met there after training for a good glass of beer'. The heavy weapons platoon would sometimes sneak away from 'field problems' in the farmland near Uplyme to go to the Talbot Arms Hotel. They would ritually place their heavy machine gun on the bar.

There was a Medical Detachment in Lyme Regis and most of its members were billeted in the Dorset Hotel. Sidney Hollender, from Monroe Township in New

Hotel Alexandra, Lyme Regis, where the Company officers lived.

St. Michael's Hotel, Lyme Regis. This was the Mess for the Battalion's officers.

Joe Dragotto and Ed Sackley from 'C' Company.

Jersey, who came as a replacement in December 1943, lived there. He remembers the cold grey days and the fireplaces in each room for heat. Before he came to England he had done six months training, including a course at the Surgical Technician School. After the invasion of Normandy he became clerk to the detachment when the previous clerk had been wounded by a sniper. The job, however, required typing skills. He said, 'I decided that I should learn how to type. So there and then, hidden behind one of the hedgerows of Normandy, I learned enough about the keyboard to gain the job of clerk.' He worked in the Aid Station, usually a few hundred yards behind the front line, for most of the war and went back to the US with the rank of Staff Sergeant. After the war he went to the City College of New York to major in accountancy.

Sidney Hollender remembers the 'good grace and patience' which the local British people had 'with the large number of American military people almost taking over their communities.' The only people who seemed to get annoyed were the farmers around the area, 'when our training efforts destroyed some of the crops in the fields.' The people of Woodmead Road also probably got a bit alarmed when troops practised with flame throwers in the field behind 'C'

View across Lyme Regis towards the Cobb. The wooden building in the foreground was the NAAFI canteen. It is now the Marine Theatre.

Robert Guiser outside the canteen in Lyme Regis. He had been badly wounded when serving as a wireless operator in North Africa and Sicily. He worked in the canteen in the evenings.

The River Lim where John Bistrica and others used to wash their Jeeps and other vehicles.

Company's headquarters. The Americans made maximum use of the features of the area. The Cobb, for instance, was used for training in amphibious landings. Infantrymen would jump off the western side of the Cobb in full kit. The harbour itself could not be used as it was mined.

There were, of course, times when the entire Battalion would leave for further training along the coast in Devon. First they would be taken by trucks to Weymouth where they would embark on the assault ships. After the exercise they would return to Lyme on the railway train to the station in Uplyme Road. The 16th Infantry was not involved in the disastrous 'Exercise Tiger' (see *Glossary*).

The population of Lyme Regis was about 2,700 when the 1st Battalion was there. That means about one in every five people was a young American soldier. Many friendships were formed. For seven months the soldiers enjoyed the hospitality of the local people and the warm friendliness of the pubs. Training was hard, but there was no deep fear attached to it. Accidents might happen, but there was no real enemy out there seeking to kill you. For much of the time, as winter turned to spring and the weather improved, life was pleasant and relaxed.

One popular centre was the NAAFI canteen in the wooden building near St. Michael's church, now part of the Marine Theatre. There, both British and American servicemen could meet. Several veterans have referred to the jam tarts made at the bakery in Fore Street and sold at the canteen. Entertainment was

Charmouth Road, Lyme Regis, with St. Michael's church on the left and the Old Monmouth Hotel on the right. The latter was the billet for Headquarters Company troops. Further down the road on the left is the red-brick building, now a youth club, which was used as a Mess Hall and for dances. Jimmy Cagney performed there.

also occasionally provided by the USO (United Service Organization) in the Company Mess Hall which was located in the large red-brick building just below the church in Church Street. Dances were also held there. Probably the most famous personality to come to Lyme to appear on the small stage there was Jimmy Cagney. The Regent cinema was also popular with the troops, as were the fish and chip shops. All of this, however, came to an abrupt end when Divisional Headquarters in Blandford ordered the battalion to leave. Many locals stood on the pavements watching the convoys move out, giving the soldiers cakes and biscuits as they went.

The town was ideal for accommodating so many troops. They came in November after the holiday season and there were many empty hotel and guest house rooms. Those who have corresponded with me about the town speak with great affection of both the place and its people. The town's Museum has a small display about the 1st Battalion of the 16th Infantry Regiment.

FIVE

The 2nd Battalion

The arrival of the 2nd Battalion of the 16th Infantry in Bridport was marred by a tragic accident. The troops began to move in on Saturday, November 6, 1943. Most of them had arrived on trains in Dorchester. There were also long convoys of trucks bringing in supplies from other places. One of these convoys was slowly approaching Bridport along St. Andrews Road. It was late and the young GI drivers were moving southwards at about 15 mph. They were close together and only the leading truck had its dimmed lights on. At about nine o'clock, one of the heavy trucks driven by Robert Joe James had fallen back a bit and then accelerated in the dark to catch up. In front of him was a cycle ridden by John Robert Bartholemew, a 57 year old employee of the Shell Mex and BP Depot near the railway station in Beaminster Road. Mr Bartholemew was returning to his home at Green Bank, Bothenhampton, after giving a piano lesson to the son of Henry George Chard. The truck ran into him.

The verdict on the accident was 'death by misadventure'. Both men involved were thought to have been partly responsible. Mr Bartholemew, for instance, may not have had a red rear light showing at the time. The Army sent the young

West Bay, Bridport. Company 'F' was billeted in buildings around the harbour.

West Bay looking west. Company 'F' used several of the holiday homes on the right as billets.
Eight men would live in each building.

soldier back to the US and it was said that he was imprisoned. It is not surprising that there were road accidents involving heavy army vehicles. The vehicles were large and the roads were narrow and winding. The trucks were left-hand drive. Headlights were dimmed and the roads had no signposts.

The 2nd Battalion, commanded by Lieutenant Colonel Herbert C. Hicks, Jr. was billeted all over the Bridport area. In the town itself, there was Company 'H', also the Battalion's Headquarters Company and a Medical Detachment. Company 'F' was stationed in West Bay and the two remaining rifle companies, "E" and 'G', were stationed in Walditch.

The soldiers soon settled in and got to know the small town and its friendly people. Staff Sergeant Marvin Segal from New York City said, 'The people in the shops, in the pubs and on the streets were, contrary to what we had heard about British coldness, very friendly and outgoing.' He added, 'The memories of that time are eternal.' For him and many others, it was almost like living in any small city in the USA. They shared a common language and a common goal.

Corporal Jess Weiss from Jericho, New York, of Headquarters Company, never forgot the townspeople of Bridport. His love for the English 'had its foundation in Dorset.' He was billeted in a house near the centre of the town, probably in East Street, and clearly remembers walking from his 'housed English home barracks' to a fish and chip corner restaurant in the town and 'the warmth, love and respect of the townspeople wherever we went.' Jess described his experiences on Omaha Beach in the best-selling book *The Vestibule*.

Corporal Jess Weiss and Technician 5th Grade Raymond Lepore of the Headquarters Company of the 2nd Battalion. Both took part in the first wave on Omaha Beach and Lepore, a medic, was killed. Jess Weiss wrote *The Vestibule*, in which he described his experiences on Omaha Beach during the assault.

A former member of the Headquarters Company was J. Parker Clerk of Baltimore, Maryland. Parker had been inducted into the army in 1942 and was sent to Camp Wheeler in Georgia for basic training. In May at Camp Blanding in Florida he was assigned to the 1st Infantry Division and was soon on his way to Scotland in preparation for the invasion of North Africa. He was in the Headquarters Company of the 3rd Battalion. In April 1943 he was transferred to the Personnel Section because of high casualties and took part in the invasion of Sicily in July. Two months later he had developed Yellow Jaundice and was sent to a hospital in North Africa. After his recovery he was sent to the Personnel Section in Bridport at the end of November in 1943.

He was billeted in South Mill and worked in the cricket pavilion not far away on the other side of South Street. The pavilion was demolished when the new

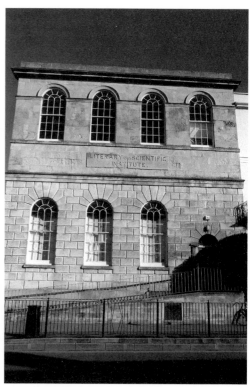

LEFT South Mill on the River Askers, Bridport, was the billet for the Personnel Section. Parker Clark remembers climbing to the second floor 'up those rickety steps in the dark of night'.

RIGHT The Literary and Scientific Institute in East Street, Bridport. This building was used by the Medical Detachment of the 16th Infantry.

Sports Centre was built. It had been similar in structure to the present Bowling Club pavilion, and was also painted green. As D-Day approached, the Personnel Office was almost closed down in order to prepare for the move. Parker spent much time playing baseball on the cricket field as well as exercising to build up his strength. During one game at the end of April he fractured his ankle badly and was sent o the US Army hospital in Axminster. When the fracture had healed, he was sent to another US Army hospital in Wales to convalesce. The hospitals near the south coast were being cleared so that they could take in the anticipated large number of casualties after D-Day. He was able to join the 16th Infantry again in Belgium.

As the months rolled by, some of the soldiers would report for Reveille from houses all over the town. While a number of romances led to weddings, other relationships developed where fidelity was tested, but many American soldiers found a 'home from home' when they were 'adopted' by families. Many

House at the end of North Allington, Bridport. Once owned by Colonel Compton, during the war it was used as a Mess Hall by the Medical Detachment.

The Real Tennis Court at Walditch which was used by the US Army for vehicle maintenance and also for dances. This unusual structure was built by Joseph Gundry in 1885 and after being completely restored is now once again being used for Real Tennis.

buildings in Bridport were taken over by the US Army. The Medical Detachment, for instance, used the Literary and Scientific Institute in East Street and a house round the corner in Barrack Street. The large house at the bottom of North Allington was used by them as a mess hall. The old Real Tennis Court at Walditch was used both for vehicle maintenance and for dances.

Food was plentiful for the army and some of it found its way to civilians. Beryl

US troops on a north Devon beach. There were training areas for amphibious landings on Saunton Sands, near Barnstaple, Woolacombe and Slapton Sands on the south Devon coast.

Bartholemew, for instance, arranged to meet Murray Horowitz outside the mess hall one evening. He came out with a large steak for her wrapped in paper. Unused to large portions of beef, she couldn't eat it. Parker Clark also managed to take meat occasionally to the home of Thomas Brownlee whom he had met in the Bull Hotel. This was after several occasions when the Brownlees had invited Parker and another GI friend to their home for Sunday lunch to share their food, restricted as it was through rationing.

The great majority of soldiers in Bridport were infantrymen and their training was very tough. Donald Wilson describes a typical day: 'Up at 0530, reveille at 0600, followed by breakfast. By 0800 we could be found double-timing on the road, stopping at appropriate intervals for callisthenics. Training continued in earnest during the day, covering the full range of infantry assault subjects – weapons, drills, demolition, camouflage, gas protection, bayonet and hand-to-hand combat and squad and platoon tactics.'

Training at the Assault Training Centre near Barnstaple was even tougher. Don Wilson described it as 'sheer hell'. The nature of the training made it quite clear that the 2nd Battalion were going to be in the first wave on Omaha Beach. They attacked fortified positions. As Wilson said, 'You don't need to know how to blow pillboxes if you come in on D-Day plus anything.' A dozen riflemen, a machine-gun squad of four, a mortar squad of four, two bazooka men, two flame-thrower men, other men for demolition and the placing of bangalore torpedoes and a radioman and a medic made up the team. Confirmation of the role they were to take was given in May when they assembled in the marshalling areas. 'We learned that we would go in on D-Day, H-Hour, 0630, first wave.'

Occasionally Don Wilson would walk along the beach below the cliffs between West Bay and Burton Bradstock with a friend, Lieutenant Siefert. They played a 'can you top this' game at targets near the cliff with their .45 pistols.

On Omaha Beach, when struggling to get out of the way of German machine gun fire, Don came across his friend lying on the wet sand, dying. There was nothing he could do to save him because of the massive chest wound. Such horrors were repeated hundreds of times on that terrible beach. In West Bay they knew it was going to be bad, but the full horror of it came to them only when they were there.

The death toll on that first wave on the beach was so great that hundreds of Dorset people were affected by the news that filtered back. Many couples had rushed to get married towards the end of May, dreaming of a happy future together. German bullets and mortars put an end to this.

At the end of May, the pleasant days in Bridport came to a sudden end. At dawn the troops climbed into trucks and began the slow journey to the marshalling areas, nearly twenty miles away. They drove through the town with

The entrance to West Bay harbour and the cliffs beyond, with Lyme Regis in the distance. Many GIs came to love this section of coast, walking east along the cliffs to Burton Bradstock.

heavy hearts. In his memoirs, Donald Wilson described his feelings on that May morning: 'I recall a particular sadness as we left. It was a deeper, more painful feeling than when I left Penn Station in New York a couple of years before. I would miss the little harbour, the quaint cottages with their tiny gardens, the West Bay Hotel with its piano and dart board 'Above all I would miss the British people, young and old, who treated us so well.'

Another beach, another day.

SIX

The 3rd Battalion

The 16th Infantry suffered heavy casualties in North Africa and Sicily. When the regiment returned to England replacements were sent to companies where they were needed. One of these replacements was John Sweeney from Oak Park, Illinois. He was inducted at Fort Sheridan, Illinois, and after basic training was sent to England. He disembarked from HMS *Maloja*, an auxiliary warship, at Avonmouth in December 1943.

With other replacements he was taken by truck to Pheasey Farms at Great Barr, near Birmingham. Pheasey Park Farm and a nearby housing estate had been commandeered by the US Army 4th Replacement Battalion, which was part of the 10th Replacement Depot at Whittington Barracks, Litchfield. The 'farm' now forms part of the Collingwood Centre. Soon afterwards he was allocated to the 16th Infantry and sent to Dorset to join the 3rd Battalion, Company 'L' at Long Bredy. The CO of the 3rd Battalion was Lieutenant Colonel Charles T. Horner. Sweeney was a member of the 3rd Platoon.

About two hundred men were accommodated in Nissen huts and wooden buildings just to the north of the drive to Kingston Russell House. The cookhouse was brick-built. Canadian troops had been there previously. The camp was partly concealed by large beech trees. One of the huts served as Company Headquarters and there was an open space used for formations at Reveille and Retreat.

To these young Americans this remote picturesque valley with its green hills and swift-flowing chalk streams was completely different from Sicily and North Africa. For some of them it was too remote, but others appreciated the quiet valley. Woodrow Rasnick, for instance, who came from the foothills of the Cumberland Mountains in Virginia, said, 'It was beautiful. I never forgot how green the fields were. I was raised on a farm, so I noticed things that city boys didn't.' Woodrow was in 'I' Company which was based just down the lane from Long Bredy in Litton Cheney.

Apart from daily training there was not much for them to do in this small village. The nearest pub was the White Horse at Litton Cheney. They did have a small canteen in Long Bredy village hall which was run by Mrs Vestey of Kingston Russell House and other local women. Most of them spent their free time in Weymouth. 'That was like leaving the farm to go to the big city,' said

Some of Company 'L' at Long Bredy. From left to right: Thomas Oates, not known, Sgt. James Wells (later killed in Hürtgen Forest and awarded DSC), J.Minetree, not known, G. Leatherwood. John Sweeney is kneeling on the right.

The White Horse Inn, Litton Cheney, was popular with troops from 'I' and 'L' Companies.

Long Bredy village hall, adjacent to Long Bredy House. This was used as a canteen by 'L' Company and occasionally for dances.

another replacement infantryman, Steve Kellman from Wausau, Wisconsin. He was in the 1st Platoon and Vincent McKinney was his Platoon Sergeant.

The GIs here did not have much contact with the village people, although Steve Kellman and others did get to know the village Special Constable, Harry Parks. He regularly walked down to the camp to chat. Some of them also became friendly with some British troops who were based nearer the coast.

Woodrow Rasnick became friendly with Michael Shea and his wife who ran the White Horse. 'When we got our rations, I would take the cigars to Mr Shea and the candy bars to his wife. I enjoyed that more than keeping it for myself,' he said. The Americans also invited British troops to share in their Thanksgiving dinner in November 1943.

When Woodrow sailed on the assault ship he spent the evening on the deck making up 'the TNT demolition charge for my crew the next morning'. The following morning all five of the landing craft used by 'I' Company were sunk. The men were rescued by Coast Guard patrol boats and those who were not wounded went in on other landing craft.

There was a bus service to Dorchester from Litton Cheney run by Freddie Pitcher. It was used for transporting livestock on market days, and calves and crates of chickens would sometimes be carried at the back of the bus. Americans often used

The Methodist chapel at Litton Cheney. It was behind this building, near the 'Triangle', that some of 'I' Company were accommodated. The chapel had an extension which served as a canteen. There were other huts in the field behind the village school.

the service and their extra weight made it impossible for the bus to climb the steep hill to the main Dorchester road, forcing them to get out and help push.

Many of the 3rd Battalion were to become heroes on D-Day and in the battles that followed. The fact that they were the first wave on *Fox Green* meant that rapid decisions had to be made. With so many officers killed, exceptional leadership was called for from those who remained. Two names in particular will be mentioned.

First, Captain John R. Armellino, commanding officer of Company 'L', who was later to become mayor of West New York, New Jersey. His Company had already been recognized for its bravery in Sicily. His son continues the story: 'My father's Company landed with the first wave . . . After leading his men across the beach my father directed the capture of a German defence position before being injured by shrapnel from an anti-tank grenade. For his heroism, he was awarded the Distinguished Service Cross and the Purple Heart.' His Company received the Presidential Unit Citation. After spending the night on a wrecked LCI with

Lieutenant Jimmie W. Monteith of 'L' Company, from Low Moor, Virginia was awarded America's highest award, the Medal of Honor. The right hand pictuure, taken by John Sweeney, is of his grave in the cemetery at Omaha Beach..

other wounded soldiers, including John Sweeney, they were both evacuated from the beach and taken back to hospitals in England. Armellino remained there for six months and his leg had to be amputated. Sweeney returned to his unit after they had 'patched him up'.

Jimmie W. Monteith from Low Moor, Virginia, was a popular officer at Long Bredy. On D-Day he was in command of 'L' Company's second assault section. They landed on *Fox Green*. His Medal of Honor citation states: "Without regard to his own personal safety he continually moved up and down the beach reorganizing men for further assault. He moved over to where two tanks were buttoned up and blind under violent enemy artillery and machine-gun fire. Completely exposed to the intense fire, First Lieutenant Monteith led the tanks on foot through a minefield and into firing positions. Under his direction several enemy positions were destroyed. He then rejoined his Company and under his leadership his men captured an advantageous position on the hill. Supervising the defence of his newly won position against repeated vicious counter-attacks,

The sweep of Chesil Beach extends to the island of Portland. The US invasion fleet sailed from Portland Harbour and Weymouth Harbour on D-Day. On the hill in the foreground is St. Catherine's Chapel, once part of the medieval abbey.

he continued to ignore his own personal safety.' He was killed by enemy fire.

The *Stars and Stripes* reported that as the personnel waded ashore, 'total casualties reduced the Company's strength from 187 to 123 men.' It was a time of great slaughter, but the 16th Infantry 'turned threatened catastrophe into a glorious victory for the American Army' winning for itself a Distinguished Unit Citation from the War Department.

Company 'L' landed on the wrong beach. From the sea it was difficult to identify *Fox Green* accurately. Steve Kellman was a rocket grenade man and he was pleased when the coxswain of his landing craft took them right up the beach 'in water only knee high'. Many other 16th Infantry men had been dropped in deep water and with their extremely heavy kit, some had drowned. Steve was part of a team trained to demolish pillboxes and he carried an aluminium ladder to cross tank ditches. As soon as he realized that the beach was not the one they had studied so closely in the marshalling area, he rid himself of the ladder and made his way to a bluff that gave some protection from the heavy enemy fire. Within minutes he was hit by shrapnel from a German 88. After twelve hours he was evacuated to an LST and received medical attention.

Eventually he was taken across to Weymouth and then to a hospital near Bristol. He rejoined his company some months later and was again wounded in

Company 'K' was stationed in Abbotsbury. It was accommodated in Quonset huts
on the hill beyond the mill pond in front of and behind the building below the church which
served as their Mess Hall.

the same leg during an effort to close the Falaise Gap. After recovering from
these wounds he was assigned to non-combatant duty and ended up in Versailles
at SHAEF Headquarters. There he met his future wife Mary, the daughter of a
British soldier.

Company 'L' and other companies of the 3rd Battalion pushed inland and took
the village of Le Grand Hameau. Some joined up with 2nd Battalion troops near
Colleville-sur-Mer. It was originally intended that Company 'K' would be kept
as a reserve unit, but when the full situation was appreciated, it went in and
joined those struggling on the beach. Captain Everett L. Booth, the CO of
Company 'K' was awarded the Distinguished Service Cross.

SEVEN

The Anti-Tank Company

The Anti-Tank Company of the 16th Infantry Regiment was based in Beaminster. Roger L. Julson from Madison, Wisconsin, was in the platoon which was billeted in the Red Lion Hotel in Beaminster's Square. He was drafted in January 1943 and inducted into the army at Fort Sheridan, Illinois. After a short basic training at Camp Hood in Texas, he was taken to Camp Patrick Henry near the embarkation port of Newport News in Virginia. He sailed on the SS *America* with 8000 men to Casablanca where he was assigned to the 1st Infantry Division. Shortly afterwards he was taken to Sicily on an LST and assigned to the Anti-Tank Company.

He, along with other new infantrymen, was kept 'on alert in a staging area' away from the fighting. They slept in 'pup' tents, which were small two-man bivouacs. About this time the Division confiscated a truckload of twelve bass accordions and Roger was given one. He kept it with him throughout his stay in Beaminster and France until he got a better one in Germany. He was able to take it around with him because his company moved about in half-tracks.

In November 1943 he set sail again from Sicily to England and was taken to Beaminster. 'Our platoon stayed on the second floor of a hotel – The Red Lion – in a dance hall converted to barracks. Other platoons were in similar buildings converted to barracks in the same village.'

They fired their anti-tank guns occasionally on army ranges away from Beaminster. Every day and some nights they were training or on exercises. If they used their half-tracks six or eight of them would sit in the back and the sergeant and driver in the front. They towed a 57 mm gun with a long barrel which required at least six men to operate it.

As is often the case, it is the trivial things that remain in the memory. Roger Julson, for instance, remembers particularly the toilet facilities on the landing craft which took them and their equipment across the Channel. 'This landing craft was open topped with about three or four foot high side rails. To go to the bathroom you climbed to the outside of the rail where there was a two foot wide ledge, hung on for dear life with one hand, did your duty in a pail with a rope attached to the handle and then emptied it into the ocean and caught a little water in the pail for the next guy.'

The Anti-Tank Company went ashore at about 1330 hours. The landing craft

Members of the Anti-Tank Company outside the Red Lion Hotel in Beaminster. Back row: John Macracken, Robert Radcliff, Jules de Vuyst, Frank Rocci, Theo Calvin. Front row: John Bataloski, Edward Stengel, Roger Julson, Hobart Williams, John Fisher. They are wearing Class 'A' uniforms and medal ribbons.

The photograph below was taken at the back of the Red Lion Hotel and is of the same group wearing ODs ('olive drab') uniforms.

LEFT A 16th Infantry half-track in France. This was like the one Roger Julson travelled in.
RIGHT The 57 mm anti-tank guns of the Company at Vettweiss.

lowered its ramp and the men went ashore in the half-tracks. Because of congestion on the beach they soon had to stop behind the Jeeps and trucks. 'German artillery and mortar fire was coming toward us frequently. We dug some trenches next to our half-tracks for some protection.'

Julson's Company had two killed and fourteen wounded. He himself 'got one piece of shrapnel that tore a hole in my legging, but just barely marred my skin.' Eventually, they were pushing inland after 'a very scary and hectic day – June 6, 1944.'

Members of Anti-Tank Company preparing for a Retreat formation, which were held daily at about 5 pm in the Square at Beaminster. People from the town used to stand and watch them.

LEFT Roger Julson and his wife Verna.
RIGHT Alice and Demetrius Lypka after their wedding at St.Mary's church, Beaminster.
His best man was Staff Sergeant Leeward Stockwell and the Rev. J.H. Stonehouse
took the service. They had a honeymoon in Lyme Regis.

Near to the Red Lion Hotel was a 'milk factory' which made dried milk during the war. The production process included rolling the powder under pressure and this left the steel rollers encrusted with thick creamy solid milk, very similar to 'Milky Bars' sold today. Local boys, like Edwin Cooper, collected 'milk sticks' from the rollers and took them to Americans living in the Red House in North Street and in the Red Lion Hotel. They received other 'goodies' in exchange.

At times there was almost a surreal atmosphere in the town. Here were large numbers of young Americans training earnestly for combat, but regularly breaking off to swap 'milk sticks' or joining the queue for fish and chips, or walking the lanes and footpaths around Beaminster, such as the popular one up to Higher Langdon, with local friends to gaze on the scene that the fictitious Tess saw when she walked over to Emminster in Hardy's *Tess of the D'Urbervilles*.

In the United States before embarkation there were many rushed marriages. Some were planned, but it was not possible to go through with them because of the urgent need for troops in Europe and elsewhere. Roger Julson of the Anti-Tank Company was engaged to Verna Paull at the time he was drafted into the army. She went to visit him at Camp Shenango near Sharon in Pennsylvania so that they could be married. Within hours of her arrival he was on his way to the port of embarkation in Virginia. They were married after the war and now live in Waukesha, Wisconsin.

ABOVE Corporal Edward Stengel and Technical Sergeant Percy Stengel (USAAF). It was Percy who ironed Evelyn's wedding dress when he was visiting his brother.

LEFT Evelyn House, a Land Girl, wearing her fiancé Roy Gunning's RAF badge next to the Land Army badge. The American is Sgt. John Byrne, a friend of the family.

Demetrius Lypka from Leibhardt, New York, was a member of the Headquarters Company 'I and R' platoon and heavy machine-gunner for Joe Rowley. He met his fiancée, Alice Rishton at a Land Army dance in Bridport. They were married at St. Mary's Church in Beaminster on May 13, 1944 – about three weeks before D-Day. Her father gave her away and Jessie Heath of the Women's Land Army was bridesmaid.

Alice worked at Bingham's Farm, Melplash, and so it was easy for her and Demetrius to meet in the evenings. Melplash is less than a mile from the camp at Parnham House. The story of their determination to meet after the wedding when Demetrius was in the marshalling area will be told later (see page 67). They now live in King, North Carolina, about thirty miles from Virginia.

Some engagements ended in sadness. Warren J. Grubner, also of Headquarters Company, was friendly with the Bowditch family who lived in Pattle, Beaminster. He fell in love with Daveen Bowditch and they arranged to marry at St. Mary's Church on June 7, 1944. When he sailed for Normandy, he did not know that he would never see her again. He was badly wounded and eventually sent back

Edward Stengel, Cora Gunning, Jules de Vuyst and Kathleen Gunning outside
the Greyhound Inn in the Square, Beaminster.

to the United States, and for two years was seriously ill in hospital. Daveen and
her family unsuccessfully tried to contact him, but eventually assumed that he
had been killed. In 1999 he returned to Dorset, but was not able to see her.

Other Land Girls married servicemen during their time in Dorset. Evelyn
House, for instance, married Roy Gunning, son of the proprietors of the
Greyhound Inn in Beaminster, who was in the Royal Air Force. Roy's sisters,
Kathleen and Cora made many friends with the young Americans. When Roy
and Evelyn married, the brother of a GI ironed her wedding dress. He was Percy
Stengel, who was in the 8th Army Air Force and was visiting his brother Edward.
As with other pubs and homes in the town, spare food was often given to the
Gunnings by the Americans, including luxuries unheard of in a nation living on
rations: sliced turkey, grapefruit juice, dried fruit and butterscotch.

Beaminster had more public houses and hotels during the war than it has
today. The Star, for instance, in Fleet Street was one which was popular with
both GIs in Beaminster and American sailors from Weymouth. The Greyhound
in the Square was also popular.

A signed photograph sent to Bill Welsford, proprietor of the Star Inn, Fleet Street, Beaminster. The men are from the US Navy in Weymouth and the picture was taken near to the Pavilion. I asked Donald Wilson about the American sailors coming to Beaminster from Weymouth. He said that the Navy and Coast Guard would travel great distances to the remotest of places to find a girl! He then added, 'The army weren't like that, of course!'

The guidon, or pennant, of the Anti-Tank Company

EIGHT

Cannon Company

The Commanding Officer of Cannon Company in Beaminster was Captain Thomas 'Obie' O'Brien. He was admired and respected by his men. During the conflict he was awarded the Distinguished Service Cross for his bravery. It was a tragic loss when he was killed near the German town of Hamich.

Foster B. Hammers was a member of Cannon Company and he lived in the Red House in North Street. The detailed account kept by him of his service in the army shows what happened to most of these young Americans who fought over here. It was a complicated process.

In October 1940 he registered for draft at Bledsoe in Harlan County, Kentucky. About nine months later he was given a medical examination at Greenville, Muhlenberg County, Kentucky and passed '1-A'. After having a further medical examination at Fort Knox, Kentucky, he was accepted as suitable for military duty.

At the end of January 1942 he reported at Fort Benjamin Harrison, Indiana, and took the oath of allegiance. He was now in the army. By the beginning of February 1942 he was doing basic training at Camp Wheeler in Georgia and three months later he joined the 1st Infantry Division for further training at Camp Blanding in Florida. Just over a week later he was moved north again to Fort Benning, Georgia, and preparations were made for overseas duty. By June he was at Fort Indiantown Gap ready for embarkation. 'All Regimental and Divisional insignia were removed' and all uniforms were handed in and replaced 'by woollen OD shirts, pants and field jacket'. On June 29, 1942, Cannon Company was activated with 88 enlisted men. Thirty more joined them before they sailed for Britain in August 1942 on the *Queen Mary*.

Hammers wrote that Beaminster was a 'nice small town to be in and conditions in England were totally different from the previous year.' Soon after their arrival in Dorset, Cannon Company was issued with six 105 mm howitzers and they were fired on ranges near Braunton in Devon. The rest of the time was spent in continuous training for the invasion. When the list of men in Cannon Company who sailed from the USA is compared with the names of those who returned to England from Sicily, only about 45 of the first list are included in the second. Most of the eighty or so not listed were casualties in North Africa and Sicily.

The 105 mm howitzers were towed by Dodge M-37 weapons carriers. For the

The Red House, North Street, Beaminster. Members of Cannon Company were billeted here. The Company Orderly Room was on the ground floor.

The house near the top of Fleet Street where other members of Cannon Company were billeted. Just beyond the house was the motor pool. Next door was the Egg Depot (now Abbot Brown & Sons) which was also used as a billet.

A DUKW amphibious truck. Cannon Company used vehicles like these. Some were parked in the motor pool at Newtown.

invasion the howitzers were carried on amphibious DUKW vehicles.

The weapons carriers and some DUKWs were kept in the motor pool at the top of Fleet Street. Vehicles were also parked in the grounds of Whatley Mill. The garden was covered with gravel. Next to the mill was the hostel for the Women's Land Army. The Land Girls had to step back into the hedge when the large 'ducks' drove down the narrow lane alongside the cemetery.

Bruce LaRose from Bethlehem, Pennsylvania, is a tough veteran who suffered much in the war and has suffered serious illness since. He is 'still very brazen, bold and outspoken', but adds 'What the hell, it's my nature.' Behind the tough exterior of an infantryman who fought through seven campaigns is a warm, witty and generous heart.

He was initially an infantryman in 'B' Company of the 1st Battalion in North Africa. He had joined the 16th Infantry in 1940 at Fort Jay on Governors Island, New York. He was 'a buck private' and along with all privates, referred to as 'yard bird', 'Dog-face' or 'Doggie'. During the invasion of Sicily he was taken into Cannon Company as a replacement. This sudden transfer was the result of him and two 'buddies' being tricked by some other GIs so that they arrived back too late for embarkation with 'B' Company. Cannon Company had sustained

Bruce LaRose of Cannon Company with his mother Florence shortly after
returning from Europe where he had just spent six months in hospital after
being severely disabled in the Hürtgen Forest.

heavy losses during the North African campaigns.

After the invasion of Normandy, as a result of the 'liberation' of wine from a
French house near Colleville-sur-Mer, he had an encounter with an officer of
Cannon Company and was sent back to an infantry company. This time it was
'E' Company of the 2nd Battalion. He stayed with them for the rest of the war
until he was severely disabled in the disaster in the Hürtgen Forest
(Hürtgenwald), a battle which was far worse than Omaha Beach. During his stay
in Beaminster he was in Cannon Company.

Along with other 'cannoneers' he was billeted in a house in a street off the
Square. He remembers that they were not allowed to use any of the possessions
of the owner of the house. They even had to store the mattresses and replace
them with army straw ones. In Hogshill Street, (then known by local people as
White Hart Street), he remembers seeing a large empty tin of Spam in a shop
window. There was nothing else there, just the empty tin. As one wartime
resident of the town said, the meat ration often consisted of a few slices of Spam
taken from a large tin. The butcher's shop is still there.

In a letter written to his sister from 'Somewhere in England' in February 1944 he wrote: 'I saw the picture 'Five Graves to Cairo' last night. I enjoyed it very much, even thought the 'theater' wasn't exactly of the Deluxe type. I guess I'm used to this life by now though.

I've worked pretty hard all day. 5.30 am to 6 pm is quite a bit of time, isn't it? I'm tired and it's time to 'hit the hay'. Please write soon and often.'

One evening Bruce and two friends decided to go to the cinema in Crewkerne. There was no transport and as privates they had no access to a Jeep, so they walked the six or so miles over the downs. As they approached the cinema, Bruce saw a young woman smartly dressed in ATS uniform getting down from a truck. He spoke to her and they all went to the small cinema. When the show had ended the three had the long walk back. Bruce had arranged to meet the young woman, Barbara Hewitt, the next evening. His two friends declined the invitation to walk with him. He also arranged to meet her the third night and Barbara took Bruce to meet the couple she was billeted with. The man was unfriendly and spoke out against Americans in general.

On his arrival back in Beaminster after dark, Bruce had little sleep because, unknown to him, the transfer to the marshalling areas was to take place early in the morning. He did not see Barbara again. As time passed, he forgot her name

Envelope containing a letter sent by 'V' mail by a man in Cannon Company. GIs would fill in a printed form with their letter and other details. When it had been checked by an army censor, it would be photographed along with hundreds of other letters. The film was then flown to the US and the photographs were developed, printed and delivered.

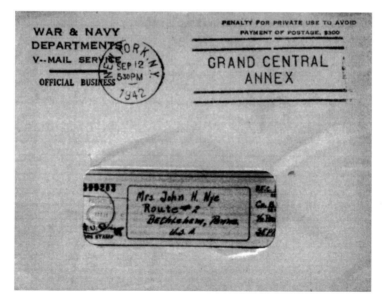

Staff Sergeant Bruce LaRose can be seen second from the front on the right. The photograph was taken on January 16, 1945 near Faymonville, Belgium, during the Ardennes Offensive (the 'Battle of the Bulge'). He is carrying extra rockets above his right hip.

until many years later he was watching a TV programme when the same name was used. He made efforts to contact her and found that she was married and living in Wareham. On a trip to Europe he arranged to go and visit her and her husband, but tragically Barbara died the day before they arranged to meet. He is still in touch with her husband.

After embarkation they sailed to mid-Channel and the DUKWs were launched into a rough sea. Five out of six sank almost immediately and the crews had to be rescued by patrolling Coastguard boats. Bruce was picked up and taken to an LST (Landing Ship Tank). The last DUKW reached the beach, but the howitzer was damaged and could not be used. All the Cannon Company survivors, without their equipment, took on the role of infantrymen and pushed up towards Colleville-sur-Mer. Bruce was assigned to a machine-gun.

In later action Bruce was awarded the Silver Star. The citation reads: 'On November 27, 1944, he unhesitatingly assumed command when his squad leader was wounded and fearlessly led the assault against hostile strong-points. By his courage and aggressive example he contributed immeasurably to the attainment of his company's objective.' Amongst his other awards and decorations are the Bronze Star, the Distinguished Unit badge with oak leaf clusters and the Combat Infantryman badge.

After the war, Bruce was recruited by the Central Intelligence Agency (CIA) and worked with them until his retirement in 1968. He now lives in Loveland, Colorado. When asked about his '403 days in harm's way', he says that the Battle of Hürtgen Forest was the worst part of the war. The forest is near Aachen and straddles the border between Germany and Belgium. For many years little was said about what almost amounted to a defeat for the US Army, and official post-war publications tend to glance over the forest battle, cruelly nicknamed the 'death factory'. For about six weeks American troops from eight infantry divisions and two armoured divisions attempted to drive the Germans out of fifty square miles of steep-sided forest.

The German artillery ripped the tops off trees and branches fell everywhere. The shells exploding in the tree-tops sent shrapnel vertically downwards on the soldiers lying in the fox-holes they had dug. Charles Whiting, in his book *The Battle of Hürtgen Forest*, states that 'it was the Western Front, 1918 all over again'. The whole forest was mined. Some units were totally wiped out by the heavily defended Germans. So grim did the siituation become that some American soldiers fled from a battle that seemed of scant strategic significance.

Those that did so paid a high price. On the final day of January 1945 Eddie Slovic, from Detroit, of the 109th Infantry Regiment, was executed by a twelve man firing squad on the orders of the military authorities. All US soldiers were informed of the execution. Bruce was in hospital in Wales when he was told. Presumably it was done as a warning to others who might think of desertion.

All of this seems so far removed from the tranquility of Beaminster and walks to the cinema in Crewkerne, but this is what happened. This was the price those young men paid when the realities of war became impossible to bear.

Another member of Cannon Company who was billeted in a house in Fleet Street, Beaminster, and who speaks highly of the town is Perry Bonner from Marshall in Texas. It was, he said, 'the best time' of his life. 'They moved us into homes and our Mess Hall was in your Town Hall.'

The Public Hall in Fleet Street was used as a mess hall and also for dances. Cooking was done in a Quonset hut behind the hall, where the Yarn Barton Car Park is located now. Like most American veterans Perry remembers the fish and chips – 'the best in England.' He also found help in the Congregational Church

Sergeant Perry Bonner of Cannon Company.

in Whitcombe Road. He said. 'I went there every Sunday. I needed all the help I could get.' Above all it was the friendliness of the local people that he appreciated. 'We got on like we had been there all our life.'

One evening in the pub a Land Girl came in and ordered several 'half and half' drinks which she quickly consumed. She turned to Perry and said, 'Do you think I am good looking?' 'No', he said, after which she tried to throw him over the bar. The only other incident in a pub of a similar kind remembered by locals also involved a Land Girl, who poured beer over a GI who tried to kiss her.

Perry became a platoon sergeant in a Line Company. He was wounded in Tunisia and Sicily and, just before the end of the war, in Czechoslovakia. They took him to a hospital in north London for a time and then transferred him to the military hospital at Fort Sam in Houston, Texas.

His English sweetheart, Betty Hooper of Crewkerne, tried to visit him when he was in London, but she arrived there the day he was being flown home and could not see him. After further time in hospital he was discharged from the army in November 1945. It took some time for him to 'find his way', but he then had a successful career in Texas. He now lives in retirement with his wife in Marshall, Texas, the place of his birth, and is an active member of his local Baptist church.

Combat Infantryman Badge, awarded to Bruce LaRose in 1944.

NINE

Marshalling Areas

Training intensified towards the end of April 1944. In addition to 'field problems' and 'night problems', each member of the 16th Infantry Regiment took part in two full rehearsals for the invasion. From May 6 all troops were confined to their company areas. There were exceptions made, but these were few. Alice Rishton and Demetrius Lypka, for instance, were given three days off so that they could get married and have a short honeymoon in Lyme Regis.

The wedding took place on May 13. Soon after their return, on May 16, the order came to move out in to the marshalling areas. Beaminster was already a 'protected area' along with most of south Dorset. Free movement within the area was allowed only to local residents, university students and those with close relatives there. Anyone trying to move into the area without police permission was liable to arrest.

Elizabeth Windmill, a worker at the Clark's Shoe Factory in Street, wanted to visit Beaminster on holiday. On arriving in the town on May 12 she reported to the police station and permission to stay was refused. She was told to leave the area. Two days later she was seen by a policeman in Tunnel Road and when she could not give a satisfactory explanation for being there she was arrested. On May 22 she appeared before the court in Bridport and was fined £5, more than a week's wages in those days. Her offence was contrary to the Regulated Areas (No.2) Order (see *Glossary*). She could have been sentenced for up to three months in prison for what she did, or fined £100.

Then the soldiers began to move out from the Company areas, their seemingly endless lines of trucks watched by the local people. Some brought biscuits and cakes that they had baked to give to the men. Some were weeping. Already the roads and lanes of Dorset had been choked by rows of parked trucks, Jeeps, tanks, half-tracks and DUKWs. There were literally hundreds of miles of vehicles, all of which had to be controlled by British and American military police. American dispatch riders constantly moved up and down the roads and field security police wearing green armbands sought to prevent the troops from talking to civilians who stood watching these lines of slow-moving vehicles, which often came to a complete halt.

At Long Bredy Hut, at the junction on the high part of the Bridport to Dorchester road, there was a major Road Convoy Regulating Point. The reason

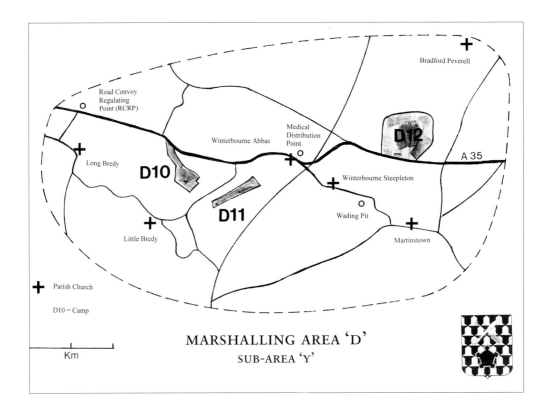

Road Convoy
Regulating
Point (RCRP)

Bradford Peverell

Winterbourne Abbas

Medical
Distribution
Point

D12

A 35

Long Bredy

D10

Winterbourne Steepleton

D11

Wading Pit

Little Bredy

Martinstown

Parish Church

D10 = Camp

Km

MARSHALLING AREA 'D'
SUB-AREA 'Y'

for the choice of the location of this control point was obvious. 1st and 2nd Battalion convoys would be approaching from the west, 3rd Battalion convoys would be grinding up the steeps hill from Long Bredy and Litton Cheney and further convoys carrying some of the troops and equipment of the 29th Infantry Division would be coming from Devon; (most of the 29th, however, sailed from Devon and Cornwall),

The 16th Infantry Regiment was heading for three camps just west of Dorchester. Wartime maps show the precise location of the three camps, and as they lay within the marshalling area nearest to Beaminster and Bridport, it is clear that these were where the bulk of the 16th went. The largest camp was on Bradford Down, close to the main road, but completely hidden from it by a band of woodland. The two smaller camps were near to Little Bredy and were in woodland which had good road access and hard tracks concealed by the trees. Area D10 is known as Well Bottom Wood and was probably used by troops from the 1st Battalion. Big Wood was area D11.

Woodland areas like these all over the county were used for the storage of large quantities of ammunition. In nearby Winterbourne Abbas there was a Medical Distribution Point, whilst below Bradford Down there was a Sterilization and

Bath Unit. Further along the road from Winterbourne Abbas to Martinstown there was a 'wading pit', a deep pool which was used for testing the water-proofing of vehicles. One of the first things the drivers had to do on arriving at the camps was to fit air pipes to the carburettor air intakes so that air was drawn in well above the water level anticipated. Joe Rowley said that he had to attach his several times to get it right. He eventually discovered a tiny pinhole in the pipe.

The vehicles were mainly parked outside the actual camps, although many were left on the farm road going across Bradford Down, past New Barn and down to Bradford Peverell. It was along this stretch of road that Demetrius Lypka was waterproofing his Jeep with Joe Nachman when he saw a train stopping at a small station in the Frome valley below. At that stage he did not know where the train was going, but he assumed there would be a phone at the station. He left Joe and went down the winding farm road to the village below and across to the station where he found a phone box.

Alice and her parents were still staying at the Greyhound Hotel in Bridport after the wedding. Demetrius phoned the hotel and Alice's father came to the phone. He sent for Alice. While the two of them were talking a train came into the station and he heard that it was going to Bridport. He quickly cut short his

The ford crosses the Winterbourne stream between Winterbourne Steepleton and Martinstown. Near here there was a 'wading pit' where vehicles were tested for waterproofing.

call and jumped on the train. The station was probably the Halt, now disused, between Bradford Peverell and Stratton. This picturesque line to Bridport was closed many years ago. Evidence of sections of the track can still be seen at Maiden Newton and Powerstock Common. The little station at West Bay and a crossing at Bradpole have been restored. Bradford Down is the only marshalling area camp which is within sight of the Bridport railway line.

When he met Alice and her mother and father at Bridport station, her parents went ahead up East Street looking for military police. The road was clear and Demetrius and Alice spent the evening together. Eventually they asked the time of the last bus to Dorchester and were told that it had gone already. He decided to hitch-hike. Not far along the road a Jeep stopped to offer him a lift. There were four MPs in it and Demetrius was questioned. He pleaded not to be turned in, but they handed him over to his CO at the Bradford Down camp. The CO was so busy that he said, 'Lypka, I don't have time to bother with you now, but don't you leave this area again.'

The next night, encouraged by his luck on the night previous evening, he persuaded some other MPs he knew to give him a lift to Bridport. After spending the evening with Alice he borrowed her bicycle and rode the twelve or so miles back to the camp. His fitness enabled him to cycle along this high road with steep hills without any difficulty. Near to the camp he left the bicycle with the men of a British searchlight battery who told him they would return it to Alice on the train. She cycled over to see Demetrius a few times until the camp was sealed. Alice was also fit as a result of working as a Land Girl. Demetrius had more freedom than most GIs because he was in an 'I and R' platoon and had to service and prepare his Jeep, which was parked outside the actual camp.

Further confirmation that Bradford Down was the main marshalling area camp of the 16th Infantry was provided by John Sweeney of 'L' Company. He remembers the night of May 27/28 when there was an air raid over Weymouth. From Camp D12 on Bradford Down he heard the air raid sirens and went with Thomas Oates to the high point of the camp on the top of the ridge near to the Dorchester-Bridport road and they looked across towards Weymouth and Portland. They could see the flashes and hear the explosions about six miles away.

Luftwaffe records state that, 'Between 0100 and 0115, 28 bomber aircraft struck the docks of Weymouth and 60.5 tonnes of high explosives were dropped – but the town of Weymouth was not badly hit'. A further 38 aircraft dropped mines at the same time on the harbour between Portland and Weymouth. For KG2, the Second Bomber Group (see *Glossary*), this was the first operation undertaken for a long time without loss.

It seems clear that the Germans had no idea of what was below them. Had they

The disused platform of the railway halt near Stratton and Bradford Peverell. It was probably here that Demetrius Lypka caught the Bridport train to see his wife Alice.

bombed any of the marshalling areas, they would have killed many troops. Also, despite what the report says, they seem to have avoided the heavily defended harbour areas. This explains why most of the bombs fell away from military targets. Four hundred houses were damaged and three people were killed, mainly in the area near Melcombe Avenue, Lynmoor Road and Crawford Avenue. Only seven delayed action bombs exploded in Portland Harbour. One suspects that the Luftwaffe were eager to drop their bombs anywhere and get away. At least five of the 1000 kg bombs did not explode.

John Sweeney and some friends had another unusual experience when they were returning from Dorchester. This was before the camps were sealed and vehicles were coming and going all the time. After a few hours in the pub, they took a taxi back to the camp, a distance of about three miles. The driver commented on all the troop movements and asked them where they were going. The four young GIs suspected he was a German spy, light-heartedly at first, and challenged him. He became agitated and stopped the cab, ordering the soldiers to get out.

Once the camps were sealed, on about May 28, there was no movement in or out. The perimeters of the camps had barbed-wire fences and Military Police stood guard at regular intervals. No communication was allowed with people on the outside once the soldiers had been briefed on the coming invasion. The tension mounted as D-Day approached.

A further piece of evidence confirming that Bradford Down was the main camp used by the 16th Infantry was provided by Ron Howse of Weymouth. His hobby is searching for artefacts using a metal detector. In 1999 he was on the upper part of Bradford Down and found 31 US Army 'dog tags'. They had belonged to men of the 37th Engineer Battalion Beach Group and had been deliberately buried. One of the engineers was John Zmudzinski of South Bend, Indiana. He told me that their base was at Swansea and that they had been moved to the camp on Bradford Down in Dorset only two weeks before D-Day. His unit had become part of the 16th Regimental Combat Team (RCT) for the amphibious landing (see Appendix C). He cannot remember why their dog tags had been collected in and was delighted to be reunited with his after 55 years.

In Camp D12 the men slept in Quonset huts or tents. Everything was very basic. After the war, it was used as a Prisoner of War Camp and improvements were made to the accommodation. In some of the Quonset huts there were rubber models of Omaha Beach with every detail accurately shown. They were based on aerial photographs taken by the Air Force and information supplied by the French Resistance.

The men were issued with impregnated clothing in case of a gas attack or some kind of chemical warfare. It was unpleasant to wear. All their other clothes, including the Class 'A' uniforms, had been put into barrack bags or foot lockers. They had their hair cut short and were checked for any infections or infestations. Steven Kellman of Company 'L' remembers a disagreement at Long Bredy, just before they moved to Camp D12, when some of the men decided that they should all have short Mohawk haircuts like some airborne forces. Fortunately the situation was brought under control by an officer.

The final confirmation of their destination was the distribution of French invasion currency. Now they were ready and waiting to embark. At the end of May they began to move. In one of the most complicated operations ever conceived, the men and equipment set out for Weymouth and Portland. As they drove down the hill to Upwey they saw Portland Harbour and Weymouth Bay full of ships.

TEN

Embarkation

Embarkation took place in Weymouth harbour and in Portland harbour and a large variety of ships was used. These ranged in size from the LCVP with a length of 36 feet to the Attack Transports with a length of over 460 feet. The 16th Infantry used three large ships in particular:

1st Battalion	USS *Samuel Chase,* American Class Attack Transport
2nd Battalion	USS *Henrico,* Bayfield Class Attack Transport
3rd Battalion	HMS *Empire Anvil,* Landing Ship Infantry (Large)

Smaller ships were used by units like Cannon Company and the 'I' and 'R' Platoon of Headquarters Company. The former used *LST 376*; the latter an LCM. One of the most famous boats used in the invasion was the Higgins Boat or LCVP. It was a wooden boat, built initially by Higgins Industries to work in the shallow waters of the swamps and marshes of Louisiana. It could float in 18 inches of water. Lowered from the Attack Transports, the boat could carry 36 men with their equipment. It could sail at a top speed of 12 knots over floating obstacles. With the bow ramp lowered the troops could get off quickly. Over 20,000 of these remarkable boats were built.

HMS *Empire Anvil* had an interesting history which shows one small aspect of the complexity of organization for the invasion.. In 1943 it was built at Wilmington, Delaware, for the US Navy and named *Cape Argos*. It was then leased to the Royal Navy and renamed *Empire Anvil*. Finally, it was returned to the US Navy in 1946 and called the USS *Rocksand*.

Right up to the last minute plans were modified. When all the ships were ready in the Harbour, Warrant Officer James Lipinski from the Beaminster Regimental Headquarters had to go to Weymouth because 'there were some last minute changes'. Jim Lipinski continues, 'I had to implement the changes and get them to the many ships on which Combat Team 16 had troops. So, just before D-Day I had the unenviable task of riding around in a small boat in the harbour to some sixty or so ships of various kinds, climbing the ladders and delivering the changes in plans. I was never so tired in my life.'

All the time that these preparations were being made, the intelligence services were doing everything they could to convince the Germans that the build-up was a diversionary measure. They were trying to persuade them that the 'real' invasion would take place near Calais. Most of the German army staff were taken in by the deception.

The 1st US Army Group (FUSAG) in south-eastern England did not really exist, though the Germans were convinced it did from the false information fed to them by double-agents and by radio communications picked up by their own intelligence listening posts. The messages were sent by operators from dozens of small units all over the south-east and told of troop movements. Dummy vehicles placed all over the area added to the deception. On the rivers Crouch, Deben and Orwell, there were dummy landing craft. The main agents had the code names Tricycle, Brutus and Garbo. The army's notional HQ was at Wentworth in Berkshire. As a result of their efforts and all the other activity the German High Command thought that twenty-five Divisions in the south-east were waiting to invade in the Calais area.

Allied intelligence was much better, although there were some deficiencies. One was their failure to detect, either from German or French resistance sources, that enemy gun positions on Omaha Beach were constructed to fire parallel to the sea and not towards it. The German defensive positions first encountered by the Americans were well placed and it was almost impossible to evade their machine-gun fire. As the troops moved across the beach and up the bluffs, they were caught again by the enfilading fire.

The Allies intention had been to put these defences out of action by heavy bombing by the Air Force and a Naval bombardment. The plan failed. Many German batteries had been moved and the empty posts left as decoys. The defences were also far stronger than had been assumed and stood up to the shell-fire. Most of the bombing failed to hit the target.

As this great Armada sailed across the Channel to a rendezvous point in mid-Channel, aptly named 'Piccadilly Circus', it was under the command of the US Navy and the US Coastguard. The Coastguard, in fact, played a great part in the landing of the 1st Division on Omaha Beach. Coast Guard Captain Edward H. Fritzche was in command of the Assault Group which consisted of the ships named earlier, as well as six LCI(L)s, six LSTs and 97 smaller craft. In addition the Coast Guard provided a 'matchbox fleet' of wooden patrol boats. The sixty boats were under the command of Coast Guard Reserve Commander Alexander Stewart and were to play an important part in the directing of landing craft movements and the rescue of troops from the sea.

On board the USS *Samuel Chase*, Captain Charles Hangsterfer was given the

A DUKW being loaded onto a Landing Ship Tank in Portland harbour.
Cannon Company sailed to France on this LST.

task of announcing 'over the ship's speaker system what LCVP boat teams were to proceed to their debarkation stations'. He was pleased to be given this task, but said later, 'It is difficult to describe the trepidation that trickles through the mind and body waiting to be ordered to venture into harm's way.' There were also letters from President Roosevelt, General Eisenhower and Winston Churchill to be read out to the ship's company before the disembarkation began. Hank asked an ABC radio announcer who was on the ship to read the letters. Afterwards he received many compliments on the 'splendid job' he did reading the letters. He accepted them 'without comment'.

The *Samuel Chase* was a new ship and the LCVPs were lowered by davits with the troops in them. This was a much easier procedure than having the men climb down cargo nets into a small craft rising and falling in the rough sea. Technical Sergeant Donald Wilson on the *Henrico* described what it was like: 'The descent of thirty or forty feet into the LCVP, via rope and cargo netting, could be an experience . . . the heavy swells caused our assault craft to rise and fall dramatically and produced alternate slack and tension in the cargo net. Inevitably the time came to climb over the ship's rail, turn and begin the descent, grasping the vertical ropes to avoid having a hand stepped on, then feeling with each foot for the lateral rope. The moment of truth came near the bottom. I guess there was a six to eight foot variance from fall to rise, so the trick was to disengage from the cargo net at the precise top of the boat's rise.'

The men who took in the boats full of troops, whether US Navy or Coast Guard, did a marvellous job in most cases. Stephen Kellman of 'L' Company from Long Bredy said: 'The coxswain of our landing craft did an amazing job, getting us right up to the beach in water only knee high.' Other boats put the soldiers down in deep water and many drowned. They had no chance of swimming with their heavy packs and equipment. There were also sand bars a long way from the shore and many of the landing craft ran aground.

When they opened their bow ramp they were met with a hail of machine-gun bullets. Hank Hangsterfer remembers being puzzled when the officer in charge of his LCVP delayed opening the bow doors. Many years after, he was told that a hail of machine-gun bullets was hitting the closed door and so opening it was left until the very last minute. Many soldiers were, in fact, killed before they could get off the boats and many of the wounded were drowned between the sand bars and the shore. Donald Wilson said, 'In moving forward the water was getting deeper. When it finally reached my chin, I inflated the lifebelt which popped me above the water, from the waist up.' In a similar situation, other soldiers got rid of the newly-issued assault jackets which were weighing them down and hindering movement. Warrant Officer Lipinski 'slipped out of his equipment in the deep water' and later removed his heavy wet tanker jacket as soon as he reached the beach.

Some troops who had come as replacements and had seen no real combat before were foolish enough to stand up in the landing craft as it approached the shore. The excitement was intoxicating and the situation unreal. It was as if they were watching a film. Many were cut down with machine-gun fire. Later, when the survivors reached the beach, some walked along 'as if they were tourists'. The hardened veterans of North Africa and Sicily kept low and moved fast.

The night before D-Day the 6th of June was stormy at sea. When they began the landings hundreds of soldiers were seasick and many were drowned. It was the weather, however, which was a factor in the success of the invasion. Field Marshal Rommel, for instance, went home on June 4 to Herrlingen to see his wife and family because he thought the invasion would not take place in such conditions. His wife's birthday was on June 6.

ELEVEN

Omaha Beach

On April 22, 1944 Field Marshal Erwin Rommel sent an order to his troops who were defending the west of Europe. It ended with the words: 'The enemy must be annihilated before he reaches our main battlefield.' When the 16th Infantry landed on Omaha Beach, for them annihilation was a real possibility.

Force 'O' (= Omaha) consisted of the 1st Division and units from the 29th Infantry Division, which was placed under 1st Division command for the landing. The 29th Division, known as the 'Blues and the Greys' was a National Guard Division drawn mainly from southern states like Maryland and Virginia. There was some rivalry between the regular 1st Division and the 'weekend soldiers' of the 29th Division, but to what extent this was justified is uncertain. The 29th did not have the battle experience of most of the 1st Division, but the latter did have many replacements for D-Day who had no more experience than the National Guard troops. It was said that the 29th gave the impression that they did not to want to learn from the 1st Division during the assault landing training in Devon. The 4th Infantry Division, who were to land on Utah Beach, also regular army, did take advantage of this opportunity. For whatever reason, the 29th Division did suffer the most casualties on that terrible day. Company 'A', for instance, lost 60% of its men in the first 20 minutes of the battle. Companies 'E' and 'F' also lost more than 40% of their men.

Casualty figures given for D-Day vary, but the following are probably as accurate as any:

	Killed	Missing in Action	Wounded	Total
Other troops	148	56	656	1373
29th Division	280	896	1027	2203
1st Division	124	431	1083	1638
Total	552	1896	2766	5214

In Winston Churchill's second statement on Tuesday, June 6, to the House of Commons he said, 'The passage of the sea has been made with far less loss than we apprehended. The resistance of the batteries has been greatly weakened by the bombing of the Air Force and the superior bombardment of our ships quickly reduced their fire to dimensions which did not affect the problem.' That may

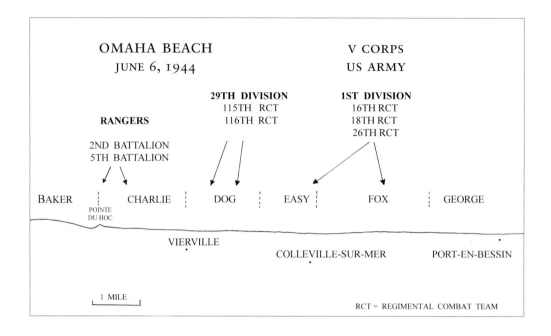

OMAHA BEACH
JUNE 6, 1944

V CORPS
US ARMY

29TH DIVISION
115TH RCT
116TH RCT

1ST DIVISION
16TH RCT
18TH RCT
26TH RCT

RANGERS

2ND BATTALION
5TH BATTALION

BAKER   CHARLIE   DOG   EASY   FOX   GEORGE

POINTE
DU HOC

VIERVILLE

COLLEVILLE-SUR-MER   PORT-EN-BESSIN

1 MILE

RCT = REGIMENTAL COMBAT TEAM

have been the case on some of the beaches, but it was not so on Omaha.

At 0635 the first wave landed on the beach. It consisted of the 16 RCT, the 116 RCT and the 2nd and 5th Rangers Battalions. The 2nd Battalion of the 16th RCT should have landed on a part of the beach named *Easy Red*, but 'E' and 'F' Companies were put ashore on *Fox Green* by mistake. The 3rd Battalion landed on *Fox Green*. Company 'E' of the 2nd suffered very heavy casualties. One of that Company, Sergeant Philip Strecyzk, was able to make a breach in the wire. He was awarded the Distinguished Service Cross for his bravery.

Communications were controlled by the USS *Ancon* and it soon became clear that things were going badly. Not only had the first wave of the attack foundered, but all of the amphibious 'Duplex Drive' tanks for *Fox Green* had sunk in the rough sea. At 0910 a report came in saying that the tide was rising rapidly and that there were still obstacles on the beach which, in theory, should have been destroyed by rockets fired from landing craft. As the water level rose the second wave of troops were held up by the first wave who were still pinned down on the beach. The unceasing heavy machine-gun fire was literally tearing them to pieces. There were also many German snipers. At 0950 it was reported that there were too many vehicles on the beach.

Roger Julson recalls the situation in his 'Memoirs'. He wrote; 'In from shore was quite a steep uphill climb, which was jammed with Jeeps and trucks. German artillery and mortar fire was coming at us frequently. We dug some trenches next to our half-tracks for some protection. I was lucky. I got one piece of shrapnel that tore a hole in my legging but just barely marred my skin.'

There were several reasons for the unexpected difficulty in getting off the beach. First, as has been said earlier, the bombing and shelling had failed to weaken the German defences. Secondly, the rocket barrage which should have torn up the wire, set off the mines and scared the Germans landed in the sea and did no damage at all. Either the aim was wrong or the landing craft crews fired them too early. Thirdly, the enemy was much stronger than predicted. Instead of there only being a badly equipped, second-rate German Infantry Division, they also faced a battle-hardened 352nd Infantry Division which had, by chance, been moved into the Colleville-sur-Mer area for beach defence exercises. Its guns positioned on the bluffs overlooking the beach dramatically increased the fire power of the enemy. It was obvious that the 352nd had not been moved there because the invasion was expected; many of the German soldiers had training bullets in their weapons. These were nowhere near as effective as proper bullets, but they were nasty. Medic Marvin Segal from the Second Battalion wrote: 'They splintered and spread out in the flesh after contact and penetration.'

It was about this time that Colonel Taylor spoke the oft-quoted words, 'There are two kinds of people staying on this beach, the dead and those who are going to die. Now let's get the hell out of here!' At 1300 the 18th Regimental Combat Team landed and at 1700 the 26th Combat Team followed them. Almost the whole of the 1st Division was now beginning to make progress inland. The 2nd Battalion of the 16th Infantry had moved up one of the three exits from the beach towards Colleville-sur-Mer and approached the village from the west. The best exit was a 10 feet wide tarmac road which went to Colleville-sur-Mer. Behind them were the smouldering remains of German strong points, pillboxes and machine-gun nests. Many more troops and vast quantities of equipment were also being moved in from the sea.

On a sunny day it could be a pleasant sight: the sandy beach about 7300 metres long with low grassy banks about 2 metres high at the eastern end and a rough stone seawall nearly 4 metres high in the west. On June 6, 1944 it was ugly. The monstrous defences and wire on the beach littered with the corpses of GIs, partly hidden by the smoke from burning grass. The fragmented German strong points, some scorched by flame throwers and the large number of enemy bodies. The bluffs and the dunes pitted with holes made by shells and mortars. The jagged steel edges of destroyed tanks, trucks and Jeeps. On the beach the dozens of medics desperately trying to help the wounded and put them back on a craft to take them to safety.

That was Omaha Beach, so far removed from the green hills and quiet lanes of Dorset where many of the soldiers, now lying dead in the sand, had spent their last seven happy months.

No mission too difficult; no sacrifice too great – duty first!
(Motto of the 1st Infantry Division of the US Army)

Semper Paratus
('Always Prepared', motto of the 16th Infantry Regiment)

*'With reverence we mourn our dead; with full hearts we sympathize
with our wounded; and with inordinate pride we salute the victorious
living of the immortal 1st Division.'*
(Congratulatory message sent to General C.R. Huebner from
General C.P. Summerall in 1944)

Appendices

In the order of precedence of the medals of the US Army the highest decoration is the Medal of Honor which was awarded for gallantry and risking life beyond the call of duty. Four men in the 16th Infantry Regiment received the award, three of them posthumously.

The second in order of precedence is the Distinguished Service Cross which was given for exceptional heroism in operations against an armed enemy.

The Distinguished Service Medal was given for exceptional achievement in duty.

The Silver Star was given for gallantry in action.

The Legion of Merit was given for outstanding service.

The Soldier's Medal was for heroism not involving conflict with the enemy.

The Bronze Star was for valour and achievement.

The Purple Heart was given for wounds received in action against the enemy.

The European-African-Middle East Campaign Medal had small bronze and silver stars added for service in campaigns.

The units in the 'Big Red One' were:
Divisional Headquarters
16th Infantry Regiment
18th Infantry Regiment
26th Infantry Regiment

Divisional Artillery
5th Field Artillery Battalion
7th Field Artillery Battalion
32nd Field Artillery Battalion
33rd Field Artillery Battalion

1st Reconnaissance Troop
1st Engineer Battalion
1st Medical Battalion
1st Signal Corps

1st Ordnance Corps
1st Quartermaster Corps.

APPENDIX C
16TH REGIMENTAL COMBAT TEAM

The 16th RCT was composed of various units which were based all over Dorset. Most of them are listed below together with the town or village they came from:

Headquarters and Headquarters Company (Beaminster)
Anti-Tank Company (Beaminster)
Service Company (Bridport)
Medical Detachment (Beaminster, Cattistock)
Cannon Company (Beaminster)
1st Rifle Battalion (Lyme Regis)
2nd Rifle Battalion (Bridport, Walditch, West Bay)
3rd Rifle Battalion (Long Bredy, Litton Cheney, Abbotsbury)
1st Engineer Battalion, Company 'C' (Studland)
37th Engineer Battalion (Swansea, Dorchester)
320th Barrage Balloon Battalion (Kingston Russell)
197th Anti-Aircraft Artillery Battalion
7th Field Artillery Battalion (Wardon Hill)
62nd Armoured Field Artillery Battalion (Piddlehinton)
741st Duplex-Drive Tank Battalion (Bournemouth)
20th Engineers Battalion (Down House, near Blandford)

APPENDIC D
RELATIONSHIPS

Many friendships and romances developed between soldiers and young women during those seven months when the 16th Infantry was in Dorset. It seems appropriate, therefore, to comment on the often repeated description of the 'Yanks' who were 'over-paid, over-sexed and over here'.

Compared to British soldiers, they were very well paid. They were young men in attractive uniforms who were outgoing and friendly. To the English girls they were like film stars and they spoke like film stars. They were also a source of 'luxuries' at a time of wartime austerity. They came here after a year of fighting in Sicily and North Africa where they had seen many of their comrades killed and were aware of the shortness and uncertainty of life.

Many of the young British men were away in the forces and so these young Americans were a disproportionate group in the population. It was inevitable that relationships would develop. Some were temporary and casual; others led to marriage. The situation then was no different from today, though the moral climate was much stricter.

GIs outside the Greyhound Inn in the Square at Beaminster.

Many of the Americans came from God-fearing communities and were influenced by them. Technical Sergeant Donald Wilson, for instance, speaks of 'a simple pleasant companionship, developing later into a very restrained romance, due to the ingrained moral and ethical codes we both shared'.

I asked Colonel Charles Hangsterfer (US Army retired) about relationships between his men and local women. He was the Adjutant of the 1st Battalion in Lyme Regis. He wrote, 'Never did I hear any complaints from the local people about anyone in the Battalion being rude or ungentlemanly, and since I would be the one who would first learn about any untoward happenings, it was one less thing to worry about.'

Several local women who were teenagers during the war have told me that the behaviour of the Americans was good. One Land Army girl described the 16th Infantry as 'gentlemen'. Even though memories can be selective, the overall impression given is that slurs of the kind we began this appendix with were unjustified in most cases.

Anne Mason was nine years old when the Americans came to Beaminster. She wrote the following words fifty-three years later:

The lorries came a rumbling into our little Square,
The American 1st Division, a sight so strange and rare.
They threw us kids gum and candy, things we'd never seen:
To us those awful war years – was it just a dream?
Our dads and brothers gone to fight – they brightened up our lives,
They made us kids feel wonderful; they made us feel all right.
We sewed their badges on for them, ran errands from morn till night,
Made dates for our lovely sisters, that got us into terrible fights...

Glossary

DEFENCE REGULATIONS. These regulations were issued in 1939, and extended in 1944, creating a 'closed' area from Lands End to the Wash which extended inland at least ten miles. This area was open only to those on 'necessary business'. This included a wide range of people from service personnel to pupils from boarding schools and students from university. The use of 'telescopes' was forbidden in this area.

DUKW. The code letters for amphibious trucks used by the US Army and commonly called 'ducks'. D = the first year of production, 1942. U = the body style, i.e. an amphibious utility truck. K = all-wheel drive. W = two rear axles. They were used for transporting men and equipment from supply ships to the beach. The maximum speed was 5 knots at sea and 50 mph on land.

JEEP. Probably the most recognizable Second World War vehicle. The Jeep was designed by the Bantam Car Company and built by Willys Overland Motors Inc. Production was started in 1940 and by the end of the war over 360,000 had been built. The Jeep of today, inspired by the original vehicle, is built by the Chrysler Corporation.

KG2. Kampfgeschwader 2, the Second Bomber Group of the German Air Force. It was an elite unit known as Holzhammer, 'Mallet'. At this period in the war they were flying Junkers 188 aircraft.

NAAFI (Navy, Army and Air Force Institute). An organization which provided catering and recreational facilities for the armed forces. Some were basic, with just a bar and a small kitchen. Others had larger cafés or restaurants and more extensive recreational and entertainment provision.

QUONSET. These were the American equivalent of the Nissen hut. They were first designed by the George A. Fuller Construction Company in New York. Production began at Quonset in Rhode Island and over 170,000 were built during the war. The basic Quonset hut was 48 feet by 20 feet. The interior could be divided up as required.

RANGERS. Elite American troops similar to British Commandos. On Omaha Beach the 2nd and 5th Ranger Battalions took part. When the units were disbanded, the troops returned to infantry regiments.

TIGER. The code-name for an amphibious landing exercise on April 27/28th 1944 in Lyme Bay. A landing on Slapton Sands in Devon was planned, but German E-boats sank two of the Landing Ship Tank, LST ships, and almost a thousand American troops were killed. The incident was kept secret for many years after the war.

Further Reading

These are some of the books I found useful for background information.

Anonymous, *The First*, (US Army). This sixty page booklet was issued to American troops at the end of the war. It was 'passed by censor for mailing home'. There are pages for autographs at the back. My copy was given by a veteran of the 18th Infantry Regiment

John W. Baumgartner, Al de Poto, William Fraccio, Sammy Fuller, *The 16th Infantry*, (Cricket Press)

Tim Kilvert-Jones, *Normandy: Omaha Beach: V Corps' Battle for the Normandy Beachhead*, (Leo Cooper)

Jess E. Weiss, *The Vestibule*, (Pocket Books). This book is dedicated to the 1st Infantry Division by the author who was in the 16th Infantry at Bridport. There is one short section about Omaha Beach

F.H. Hinsley, *British Intelligence in the Second World War, Vol. 4, Security and Counter-Intelligence*, (HMSO)

M. Howard, *British Intelligence in the Second World War, Vol.5*, Strategic Deception, (HMSO)

M. Attwood, D. Harrison, *Weymouth & Portland at War: Countdown to D-Day*, (Dovecote Press)

G. Forty, *Frontline Dorset: a County at War, 1939-45*, (Dorset Books)

Acknowledgements

I am indebted to the following people for their help in this project:

John E. Bistrica, Youngstown, Ohio; Perry D. Bonner, Marshall, Texas; J. Parker Clark, Baltimore, Maryland; Joseph A. Dragotto, New York Mills, New York; Frederick Erben, Lyndenhurst, New Jersey; William Friedman, Washington, DC; Robert M. Guiser, Newell, Pennsylvania; Sidney Hollender, Monroe Township, New Jersey;Foster B. Hammers, Madisonville, Kentucky; Charles M. Hangsterfer, New Britain, Pennsylvania; Roger L. Julson, Waukesha, Wisconsin; Stephen Kellman, Wausau, Wisconsin; Bruce LaRose, Loveland, Colorado; John H. Lauten, Camarillo, California; James B. Lipinski, Alexandria, Virginia; Demetrius Lypka, King, North Carolina; Angelo Macchi, Saint Louis, Missouri; Woodrow W. Rasnick, Birchleaf, Virginia; Joseph A. Rowley, Lakehurst, New Jersey; Marvin Segal, Hollywood, Florida; John Sweeney, Phoenix, Arizona; Jess E. Weiss, Jericho, New York; Donald E. Wilson, Lakehurst, New Jersey; John J. Zmudzinski, South Bend, Indiana.

Numerous Dorset people have also been extremely helpful. They include: John and Poppy Butcher, Weymouth; Donald and Rachel Bowditch, Beaminster; David Bullock, Beaminster; Dawn Gould, Weymouth; Beryl Hyde, Bridport; Jack and Cora Lawrence, Mosterton; Peter and Kay Lawrence, Beaminster; Cecil Poole, Beaminster; Cecilia Toohill, Bridport; Norman and Audrey Welsford, Beaminster.

My final debt is to John Bromage, Weymouth & Portland Borough Council, for kindly providing the colour photograph on the front cover.

Index

Aachen 63
Abbotsbury 11, 49
Adamcyzk, J 19
Algeria 9
Ancon, USS 76
Anti-Tank Company 50
Armellino, J.R. 46
Arzew, Gulf of 9
Avonmouth 43
Axminster 38

Baltimore 37
Barnstaple 41
Barrack St., Bridport 40
Bartholemew, B. 41
Bartholemew, R. 35
Beaminster 10, 11, 13, 21, 23, 50, 53, 65, 81
Belgium 28
Benning, Fort 18, 25
Bethlehem, Pennsylvania 8, 59
Binghams Farm, Melplash 54
Binnegar Hall 11
Bistrica, J. 18, 27, 28
Blandford Forum 11, 34
Blanding, Camp 8, 57
Bledsoe, Kentucky 57
Blues and Greys 75
Bonner, P. 14, 63
Boston, Massachusetts 8
Bothenhampton 35
Bowditch, D. 54
Bowditch, R. 13, 18
Bowers, Lt. Col. 25
Bradford Down 66, 70
Bradley, O. 16, 18, 25
Braunton 57
Bridport 13, 18, 35, 67
Brownlee, T. 41

Bull Hotel, Bridport 41
Bullivant, E. 15
Burton Bradstock 6, 41, 42

Cagney, J. 34
Calais 72
Cannon Company 8, 9, 57, 59
Cape Cod, Massachusetts 8
Casablanca 50
CIA 63
Chard, H.G. 35
Churchill, W. 73
Clerk, J.P. 37
Clyde, Firth of 9
Coast Guard 45, 72
Cobb, Lyme Regis 33
Colleville-sur-Mer 49, 60, 77
Crawford Avenue, Weymouth 69
Crewkerne 61
Culebra 8
Cumberland Mountains, Virginia 43
Czechoslovakia 86

Deery, L. 16, 23
Devens, Fort 8
Devon 12, 66
Dorchester 10, 24, 35, 45, 69
Dorset Hotel, Lyme Regis 29
Dragotto, J. 28, 29, 31
Driscoll, E.F. 25
Duchess of Bedford, HMS 9

East St., Bridport 68
Easy Red 76

Eisenhower, D.D. 13, 18, 73
Empire Anvil, HMS 23, 71
Erben, F. 27, 28

Falaise Gap 49
Fleet, St., Beaminster 10, 18, 59
Fléville 8
Fox Green 46, 47, 48, 76
French Resistance
Fresno, California 18
Friedman, W. 15, 16, 20
Fuller, S. 17
Furzy Lane, Beaminster 21, 23
FUSAG 12, 72

Gettysburg College 25
Glasgow 9
Glendale, California 18
Göring, H. Panzer Division 9
Gourock 9
Governors Island 8, 59
Great Barr 43
Greenville, Kentucky 57
Greyhound Hotel, Bridport 67
Greyhound Inn, Beaminster 55
Grubner, W.J. 54
Guiser, R. 26, 32
Gunning, C. 55
Gunning, K. 55
Gunning, R. 55

Hammers, F. 57
Hangsterfer, C.M., 'Hank' 25, 26, 72, 74, 81.
Harvard University 8

Heath, J. 54
Henrico, USS 71, 73
Hewitt, B. 61
Hollender, S 29.
Hooper, B. 64
Horner, C.T. 43
Horowitz, M. 41
Hotel Alexandra, Lyme
  Regis 30
House, E. 55
Huebner, C. 10, 78
Hürtgen Forest 63

Indiantown Gap, Fort 9
Indiana 70
Italy 10

James, J.J. 35
Jay, Fort 8, 59
Julson, R. 50, 52, 53, 76

Kellman, S. 45, 48, 70, 74
King, North Carolina 54
Kingston Russell House 43
Knox, Fort 57
Kryzanowski, S. Sgt. 21

Land Army 23, 59, 81
Langton Long, Blandford
  11
LaRose, B.A. 8, 59, 61
Lauten, J. 16, 17, 18, 20,
  24
Lepore, R. 37
Liebhardt, New York 54
Lindenhurst, New York 27
Lipinski. J. 71, 74
Litchfield 43
Little Bredy 66
Litton Cheney 11, 43, 45,
  66
Liverpool 10
Long Bredy 43, 47, 66, 74
Lyme Regis 11, 13, 18, 20,
  25, 29
Lynmoor Road, Weymouth
  69
Lypka, D. 19, 54, 65, 67,
  68

Macchi, A. 21
Madison, Wisconsin 50
Maiden Newton 13, 68
Maloja, HMS 43
Marine Theatre, Lyme Regis
  33
Marshall, Texas 63
Martinstown 67
Marvin, L. 18
Mason, A. 81
Matthews, J. 16
McKinney, V. 45
Medal of Honor 47, 79
Melcombe Avenue,
  Weymouth 69
Melplash 54
Messina, Straits of 10
Monroe Township, New
  Jersey 29
Monstrance 28
Monteith, J.W. 47
Montgomery, B.L. 13, 18

NAAFI 32, 33, 82
Nachman, J. 67
Neal, Sgt. 14
New Berne, North Carolina
  8
Newtown, Beaminster 10
New York 9, 31, 42
Niscemi 10
North Africa 9, 37, 43, 57,
  59, 74
North Street Beaminster 20

Oak Park, Illinois 43
Oates,T. 68
O'Brien, T. 57
Omaha Beach 23, 26, 41,
  60, 70, 75, 76, 77

Parks, H. 45
Parnham House, Beaminster
  11, 15, 19
Paull, V. 53
Penn Station, New York 42
Pheasey Park Farms 43
Piccadilly Circus 72
Pitcher, Freddie 45

Plitt, C. 16
Poole, C 13
Portland 69, 73
Public Hall, Beaminster 20,
  63
Puddletown 11, 13

Rangers, US 9, 82
Rasnick, W. 43
Red House, Beaminster 53,
  57
Red Lion Hotel, Beaminster
  50, 52
Rishton, A. 54, 65
Roosevelt, F. D. 73
Rommel, E. 74, 75
ROTC 18, 25
Rowley, J. 18, 67

Saint Mary's church,
  Beaminster 53
Saint Michael's Hotel, Lyme
  Regis 29
Sam Houston, Fort 64
Samuel Chase, USS 71, 72
Segal, M. 36, 77
Sharon, Pennsylvania 53
Shea, Mr. 45
Shenango, Camp 53
Sicily 9, 12, 57, 74
Slapton Sands 12, 24
Slovic, E. 63
South Bend, Indiana 70
South Mill, Bridport 37
Star Inn, Beaminster 55
Stars and Stripes 48
Stengel, E. 54, 55
Stengel, P. 54, 55
Street, Somerset 65
Strecyzk, P. 76
Summerall, C.P. 78
Swansea 70

Talbot Arms Hotel, Uplyme
  29
Taylor, G.A. 16, 17, 77, 86
Tegtmyer, C. 16
Tennant, K.S. 21
Thanksgiving 20

Three Cups Hotel, Lyme Regis 29
Tidworth, Hampshire 9
Tiger, Exercise 33, 82
Tor Cross, Devon 12
Troina 10
Tunnel Road, Beaminster 65

USO 34
Uplyme 29
Utica, New York 28

Versailles 49
Vestey, Mrs. 43
V-Mail 61

Vuyst, Jules de 55

Walditch, 36, 40
Wales 38
Walt Disney Studio 17
Waukesha, Wisconsin 53
Wareham 11, 62
Way, Mrs. 28
Warwick Castle, HMS 9
Weiss, J. 36, 37
West Bay 18, 42
Weymouth 17, 24, 48, 55, 68, 70, 71
Wheeler, Camp 57
Whitcombe Road, Beaminster 64

White Hart Street, Beaminster 60
White Horse Inn, Litton Cheney 44, 45
Whiting, C. 63
Wilson, D. 41, 42, 73
Windmill, E. 65
Winterbourne Abbas 66
Woodmead Road, Lyme Regis 13, 27, 28, 31
Woolacombe 12

Youngstown, Ohio 27

Zmudzinski, J. 70

This photograph was taken in Czechoslovakia by Joe Rowley of Headquarters Company. It shows the parading of the Stars and Stripes and the Regiment's flag. Joe used a film found in a bombed shop.

THE END OF THE ROAD

From Oran in North Africa to Elbogen in Czechoslovakia, the US Army's 1st Division had fought the German army.

At Elbogen, Brigadier General George A. Taylor, by then Assistant Commanding General of the Division and formerly the Commanding Officer of the 16th Infantry, accepted the surrender of German Lieutenant General Fritz Benicke and the 12th German Corps on May 7, 1945.